READER COMME

I received your book in it
ruined my day. I simp I
finished it late that eveni ls
I've had in a long time and deserves great success.
Ted Brewer - Brewer Yacht Design
Gabriola Island BC CANADA
www.tedbrewer.com

I have also many times told the story about "the Australian who sailed in the small boat". It differs slightly from what you writes. I think my version is somewhat better. I don´t remember that you had a sextant. Did you really told me that? I was very worried about how you should find Barbados. As I remember it you sailed in zigzag from Gibraltar to the Canaries for not to miss it.
Jan-Olof Ronn - Gothenburg Sweden
Atlantic Crossing in Costa Mera

To think of all the equipment and paraphernalia that the boats have onboard these days to do the crossing, and how little you had - Amazing achievement!
Bruce Gaynham
World Cruising Club

I thoroughly enjoyed it, particularly enjoying your style of writing and the fact that you describe places that I had visited and sailed past at about the same time as you - though I only got half way across the Atlantic and I was in a 3000 tonne surveying ship!

As one who has spent much of his time peering out of the bridge window in order to avoid running down the likes of you, I have always thought small boat ocean sailors were mad, naive or incredibly brave. Your book has convinced me that you were all three. And now you want to do some more!
Robert Ward - Captain, RAN
Deputy Hydrographer of Australia

BOOK REVIEWS
Cruising World - February 2005
Sailing Small

Bored with conventional life in Australia, Geoff Stewart wanted to do something interesting and in the freewheeling spirit of the the times, the rockin 70's, he hopped a plane to England where he bought a 22 foot Drascombe Longboat, Donna and planned to cruise the Greek islands with it. He didn't know much about sailing. In fact he knew just about nothing. But he didn't let a little thing like that stop him.

Stewart piloted his open boat across the English Channel, then banged around the canals of France before heading to the Mediterranean Sea. It was here that the idea of sailing across the Atlantic captured his fancy, or, one might say – perhaps more to the point – took hold of his sanity. He figured people had rowed across the ocean in open boats, and he concluded that it wuold probably be much easier to make the long passage to the Caribbean under sail. He decided to give it a try.

Packing the boat with provisions and water Stewart pointed the bow of his boat West making his way through the Strait of Gibraltar and out to sea, bound for Barbados. He stopped briefly at the Canary Islands and then sailed on, enduring storms and calms. Sharks followed the boat and eyed him hungrily. Slowly Stewart's provisions ran out, and things got a tad dicey. Luck favours drunks and sailors, though, because he actually made it across. And it only took 59 days. **D.W.S.**

If you're one of the many people who think there's little adventure in this world, think again. Geoff Stewart is living testimony that there is.
Cruising Helmsman - October 2004

Sail South till the butter melts
Atlantic adventures in an open boat

Sketch by Mikko

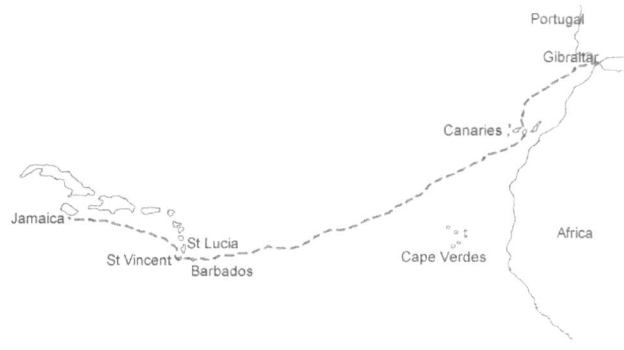

Geoff Stewart

Published by: The Continuity Company, Melbourne, Australia, 2004.

Copyright © G. W. Stewart 2004.

ISBN 0-9752328-1-9

All rights reserved. No part of this publication may be reproduced, stored in a retrieval system, or transmitted, in any form or by any means, electronic, mechanical, photocopying, recording or otherwise, without the prior permission of the publisher.

The mailing address of The Continuity Company is:
Box 211
Camberwell, Vic 3124
Australie.

Cover Images

Donna in Puerto De La Luz, Gran Canaria. Note square locker entrance in middle of boat and rowing oar brought from Australia - for use as an emergency mast - in the foreground. The lovely Kerstin who was my muse during the crossing and a shot of the author deep in a lock in the French Canals.

Back cover – the moment of departure from Gran Canaria – turn right past that groyne in the background and out into the Atlantic, Donna Elvira in the canal configuration and a note sent by the author to his mother on the day of departure.

Glossary

There are some yachty words and some esoteric words defibrillated in the glossary.

Collaboration

My thanks to Kerstin Johanssen, Jan-Olof Ronn, Nick Grainger, Peter Harris, Ron Joosten and Per Bengtsen for their insights. I should also thank all the yachties I met along the way – most of them passed on useful information, or at least an amusing story.

INTRODUCTION

This adventure gave me - for the first time in my life - the feeling that I had actually 'done' something. Most people I talk to think that heading out into the Atlantic in an open boat is something they would never do. That's OK, you don't have to. However I did and my story is laid out in the following pages.

I sailed from Gibraltar to the Canaries, Barbados, St Vincent and Jamaica in a 22 foot open boat. I needed navigational advice from a lightship while crossing the English Channel, had trouble finding the Canary Islands, but hit Barbados on the nose at the end of a 3000 mile 'Columbus' style crossing.

'Sail South till the butter melts, then due West', is the frolicsome version of the sailing directions. A more nautical version suggests sailing South until Polaris is a hand's breadth above the horizon. The 70's pot heads would head in the general direction and listen for radio Barbados. You can hear it from 500 miles out.

People always ask 'what was the worst moment'? It was heading down a large steep wave and thinking that I was going to die. It is covered in the first chapter. The next worst moment was on the way back to UK as second officer on the barquentine Regina Maris being 100 feet up in the rigging taking in sails during a 50 knot squall.

Preface to the Second Edition

In this edition I have tried to allow the sailing adventure story to flow with fewer interruptions. A great deal of the material comes straight out of the log, that preserves the immediacy, but has some discontinuities. The mind jumps around a lot when you are alone in the middle of the ocean for two months. There is also the illusion that one might solve the world's problems at a stroke. So I have undertaken some smoothing, some deletion and some clarification. My goal was and is to share the experience with you.

I have also put a chapter on the web site about preparing for an ocean crossing. www.sailsouthtillthebuttermelts.com Many cruisers have all the angles covered. However there may be some cruisers in large yachts who have not thought through the fundamentals. I must say that one friend who recently cruised for five and a half months reported that the most important issue was having a hair dryer with sufficient oomph. Even twelve volts was not enough.

Here are some fragments

'I have recently heard a horrific story of a husband and wife team who had a problem with a fitting up high on the mast. The husband winched himself up to fix it and had a heart attack while up there. He died. This leaves the wife with the job of getting the boat to harbour.

In this case she couldn't get him down and he had been rotting up there there for two weeks by the time she reached harbour.'

'How well do you know your crew. Will they keep watch in a responsible fashion? I have heard many stories of the skipper coming on deck to find the crew member standing watch sound asleep. Your life is at risk here.

How will this crew behave in a crisis? Do they have courage, discipline and tenacity? Your life may depend upon it.

What about hijack. The contemporary spoilt brats may decide to throw you overboard and enjoy the sail without you. You would not be the first or the last.'

Some of you will know all of this stuff and more. It is not you I am writing for. Not everyone will have faced up to these issues.

Whatever your voyage, I wish fair winds and kind seas.

About Drascombes

The Drascombe Story
by Ted Brewer, published in 1975

Since 1969 the Drascombe range of boats, all small, open daysailers, have made voyages that relatively few yachtsmen would care to undertake in craft much larger.

The rest of this article is on the web site
  www.sailsouthtillthebuttermelts.com

Table of Contents

READER COMMENTS 1

BOOK REVIEWS 2

INTRODUCTION 5

PREFACE TO THE SECOND EDITION 5

ABOUT DRASCOMBES 6

THE WORST MOMENT 9

IN THE BEGINNING 13

DONNA ELVIRA 24

FRENCH CANALS 29

ALAIN BOMBARD - ADVICE 37

MEDITERRANEAN COAST OF FRANCE AND SPAIN 39

GIBRALTAR 50

DOWN TO THE CANARIES 55

GRAN CANARIA 67

THE CROSSING 75

MY COOL RETURNS 81

SHARKS 92

MORE OATS 98

SINKING 105

WHERE AM I 116

CHRISTMAS EVE 128

BARBADOS	**133**
ST VINCENT	**138**
TO JAMAICA	**142**
AFTER SAILING	**147**
DOCUMENTS	**157**
GLOSSARY	**160**
PLANNING AN OCEAN CROSSING	**165**
ORDERING INFORMATION	**166**
Book Sellers	*166*
Signed copy of the Second Edition	*166*
Signed copy of the First Edition	*166*
If all else fails	*166*

The Worst Moment

People always ask, 'what was the worst moment'. Well, it was heading down a deep hole and thinking that I was about to die. I was poised in the stern looking down. It looked a long way down. I feared that Donna would spear into the base of the wave, fill with water and sink. I had been making very satisfactory progress in recent days. Suddenly, I felt that my life may be coming to an end. Not immediately. After the boat had sunk I would last a day or two in the water, or until the sharks found my odour. That wouldn't be too long, I hadn't washed for many, many days.

Holes in the ocean you ask. Well yes. Listen ... I was there. The boat was 22 feet long, this face was longer. Down we went. The wind had been a bit stronger than usual for a couple of days and the waves had built to around 20 feet. I had been reaching across the wind and waves with only two small sails up - the jib and mizzen – going as fast as little Donna could go, maybe six knots. It was exhilarating.

Jib and mizzen in Gran Canaria

On down the face of this hole. It all happened very quickly. I wasn't sure if the boat would float when it was full of water. I had loaded the boat up with all sorts of gear she would not normally carry, two anchors and basically two of everything else including rudder tiller assembly, stoves, compasses, masts, and so on. Not enough food however.

We reached the bottom of the hole. The nose went under and lots of green water came in over the bows. Then we broached (turned sideways) and filled completely with water. However Donna was still afloat! The bucket disappeared over the stern. This was my toilet bucket as well as the main bailing instrument. Yes, for those of you who are counting, there had been two, but things kept going missing.

First get the water out of the boat. I grabbed a saucepan and frantically bailed. Got most of the water out, then turned my attention to these large waves. Perhaps I should concentrate on staying afloat for the next little while. As Hemingway would say 'Il faut d'abord durer'.

To keep the nose pointing at the waves, I put out the sea anchor a canvas sack on the end of a rope. Yachties will know that the length of the line on the sea anchor dramatically affects the behaviour of the yacht. I tried different lengths. It didn't work, the boat always seemed to be lying across the waves and in danger of being rolled. I took in the sea anchor and tried a six foot length of wood transverse on the end of a line. Didn't pull so hard, but kept the bow facing the waves.

Sat in the stern and watched these 20 foot and more waves. Donna scrambled up and over this one and another and another. Not much water coming aboard, but I didn't want to risk going to sleep. I was very hungry.

I had some life boat survival cubes – small vitamin impregnated biscuits. I ate one. It was better than nothing, but somewhat less than a proper meal. I had enough of these to last perhaps a week with one per meal. My gums were starting to bleed. Throughout the voyage I had been taking a multivitamin pill every day. Since I didn't know how much longer I would be out here, I had tried taking one every second day. Didn't work - so I went back to taking one every day. I was trying to ration everything. I had been at sea for 56 days and didn't know how much further I had to go.

In fact I didn't even know if I had passed the line of Carribean islands and was headed for Mexico. Later when I saw St Vincent and St Lucia I realised that they were tall enough to be easily visible. Barbados on the other hand was 26 miles long and not very high. It was my target and it would be easy to miss.

For the next 42 hours I sat in the stern and willed Donna over each wave. Eventually the sea moderated a little, so I set the jib and mizzen and got under way. We were travelling quickly, but seemed OK. As long as I didn't find another hole. I needed to get some Westing in, make a landfall and get something to eat.

Dorado, wonderful food

Noticed a large three foot fish (Dorado) swimming next to the boat. Grasped my trident, hooked my left leg over the tiller to steer and leaned out towards the Dorado. He was just out of reach. And there we stayed. Donna was doing well. Steering with the leg worked fine. I was poised to spear the Dorado. The Dorado was keeping up with the boat, but staying just out of reach. Some fresh fish was just what I needed. I had speared a few of these before and knew that there was a risk of losing it off the end of the spear as it flailed to get free. First I had to get it onto the end of the spear. Still just out of reach.

We stayed this way for an hour and a half. Me poised. Dorado playing. Then he came within reach and I planted the spear. A quick movement forward and up and he was in the boat. Maybe the gods were on my side after all. I lowered the sails and started the stove. Didn't have any oil or butter. Chopped the large fillet off the back and half burnt, half cooked it to make it firm and ate lots. That felt better. Now lets get the sails up and make some more distance West.

Next morning I noticed a smudge on the horizon. Put my glasses on and had another look, I could still see a smudge. Cleaned them and had another look, certainly appeared to be land. I had been shooting the sun most days with my sextant, doing a Columbus style crossing without clock or radio. Perhaps this was Barbados. To hit that speck at the end of a 3000 mile crossing would be spectacular.

The next question people ask is 'why did you do it?'. That one is much harder. When asked why do you climb mountains, Hillary replied 'because they are there.' Bonnie and Clyde on why they robbed banks - 'that's where the money is.'

My answer would try to explain that it was all a bit of an accident. I originally intended to stooge around the Greek Islands. If you have read the Magus by John Fowles you will understand what I was looking for. Some gorgeous twins. I had the right boat for that expedition. Perhaps I should start at the beginning.

In the beginning

Sailing was not a big thing for me. I did the conventional stuff, played cricket, squash, golf, and tennis did a bit of recreational surfing and some skiing. My sailing experience was:
- a beam reach out and back with John Collingwood in a Gwen 12 from Davies Bay Yacht Club
- the odd race in a dingy on Lake Burley Griffin in Canberra
- To Brighton for an ice cream and back with Kenny Richardson in a Tumlarin from the Royal Yacht Club of Victoria.

However I was approaching thirty, single, living in conservative Melbourne (great place to raise your kids) and looking for some action. I had a Bachelor of Commerce from Melbourne University and had worked for IBM, Honeywell, Beckingsale Management Services and LaTrobe University. I had also run my own management consulting business and done some acting.

Dressed up by Grandma

From the age of 6 to 12 we lived on a small farm on the outer edge of Melbourne. I lay in bed until the rest of the family had departed for school and work. Then I fed the chooks and cooked my breakfast. It was a cross between fried and scrambled eggs with lots of multi coloured sugary stuff thrown in. Sweet kid food. One of my other jobs was emptying the giant canister from the outside toilet. Big job for a small kid and very messy.

Secondary schooling at Scotch College. A somewhat traditional, but valuable experience. This was when school was a place to learn stuff, grow your skills and compete. Very different to the contemporary slide into mediocrity. I was captain of the under 16 B cricket team, we challenged the A team and beat them. We won the Hoadley Hide - a state wide scouting competition. I broke the record for the junior cross country. I made the Second 11 (cricket) and the Second 18 (Australian rules football) in year 12. Not bad for a 16 year old. Some of my colleagues were two or even three years older. I tended to be one of the bottom students in the top class, an odd place to be. Chesty Bond advised 'Stewart, what you don't know about Latin would fill libraries' – still does.

I was the servant to Tony Staley's Caesar with Peter Blazey as Antony and Patrick McCaughey as Portia in the 1957 production of Julius Caesar. The best prank of this era was the nailing of a fish to the underside of a table in the masters common room. The foul smell lasted for weeks. Floorboards were taken up, cupboards were removed yet the problem remained elusive and the stench intrusive. The source was only discovered when the rotten fish fell from the nail.

Ian, Elizabeth and me

My contemporaries said that I thought too much. This was the comfortable 50's and 60's in wowserish, hierarchical, staid Melbourne. Respectable people did not talk about sex, politics or religion. Nice girls wore twin sets and pearls and were respected. Today we have crop tops, hipsters, skirts with slits, 'Sex in the City' and 'Desperate Housewives'. Not so much respect however.

Women abandoned social superiority to enter the bear pit and arm wrestle with the men. Looks pretty silly to me. Whingeing about the glass ceiling is even sillier. This is the battle you wanted girls so just shut up and get on with it.

Should have stuck to football. My mother's ambition for me was that I should play league football. Didn't do that, but did pick up 56 goals as full forward for the Old Scotch juniors.

Where was I. A meander through university. JFK was assassinated and we were going to change the world. Actually the pill changed the world, initially with an epidemic of STDs and later with lots of 'assertiveness'. Girls were sweeter then.

My father had worked in the family bakery and cake shop in Footscray that my great grandfather had started in the mid 1800's. He owned a share in the business and hoped to buy his father out. However my grandfather sold the business during the second world war and left my father unemployed.

He enlisted, became a pilot, served in Europe and went 'missing in action' to use the euphemism. My cousin has told me of the moment when the telegram arrived. My mother knew that this was the news she dreaded and would not go to the door.

We owe a very great deal to this generation who were willing to give their lives for their country. The cream of Australian manhood wiped out twice in thirty years. I wonder if Australia might have evolved differently if these men had been a continuing part of our destiny.

He flew missions from Brindisi in Italy to Warsaw during the Warsaw uprising. Eight hours over hostile territory, then coming in low and slow over an enemy held city to drop guns into the square. A gesture of support by Churchill to the Polish government in exile who were ensconced in London. You may recall that the Polish government in exile ordered the uprising in order to assert sovereignty ahead of the Russian arrival. The Russians waited on the other side of the Vistula river for the Germans to quell the uprising, then took the city. He was posthumously awarded the Polish Cross. People tell me he was a pleasant fellow, a lot like my brother they say – could be a message there. I still have some of his swimming trophies from the Footscray Swimming Club.

He didn't return from a sortie dropping supplies to the partisans in Jugoslavia. One story is that there was some confusion between imperial gallons and American gallons. They may have just run out of juice. What a waste.

One summer I was working in the bakery at Rosebud. Feeding the ovens to produce delicious fresh bread and driving around the holiday strip delivering the bread to shops. I had done a year of Commerce and two years of Medicine. I had lost my enthusiasm for Medicine. I had asked all of my colleagues why they were doing this course which took so long, some said money, some said status and others were not sure. I had dreamed of being the country General Practitioner – someone both useful and respected. Perhaps modelled on the Cordner brothers who were our local doctors at Diamond Creek. This dream had evaporated and I was lost.

I drove off into the sunset in my slow, little, side valve Morris Minor. Three days and 3000 miles later I arrived in Perth and got a job delivering bread. I was involved in a minor accident. Back at the office the accountant - a first generation immigrant - said 'tell me what happened and I will fill in an accident report'. I said give me the paper, rapidly drew a three stage diagram and added few paragraphs of text. He said 'you're a student aren't you'. He was astonished that someone would walk away from the opportunity to get a university degree. He suggested that I go back to University.

I re-enrolled in the Commerce degree over the phone and set off back across the Nullabor Plain to Melbourne as co-driver with a bloke I had just met. The car started off OK. Then it lost power and couldn't pull in fourth gear, I changed to third, it got worse, I changed to second. We ground to a halt outside a solitary pub by the rail line. We had a few drinks with the locals. I played some fragments of waltz on the piano for a couple who wanted to dance. Last I saw of the car owner, he was on a short wire rope behind an oil tanker heading for Kalgoorlie. I had to get back to Melbourne to start the University year so I jumped the train which came through at 2AM.

I had an Economic Geography lecturer who suggested that the signature ideas of the 20th Century were 'time and technology'.

Well on this little voyage I was planning to have a holiday from the obsession with 'time and technology'.

Geoffrey Blainey was my economic history professor. One of my colleagues asked if we could call ourselves economists when we graduated. Blainey hesitated, 'well yes ... in the sense that someone who plays football for Bundalaguah East can call himself a footballer'. Geoffrey does not recall this incident. However I was his young student and I remember. We were delighting in the extent to which world affairs could be understood through Economic rather than Political History.

Some would say that the French Revolution was brought on by the heavy taxes levied to pay for the French involvement in liberating America from the English. Forget about liberte, egalite, fraternite and class hatreds, it was taxes. Perhaps 'Dubya' would benefit from a history lesson – the Americans would not have gained independence without French assistance. Hold those comments about 'cheese eating surrender monkeys'.

An Anatomy professor - could have been Red Russell - advised that spermatozoa were not manufactured when in the bath due to the high temperature. There followed some experimentation with making love in the bath. More about futility than fertility.

'Pansy' Wright was my Physiology lecturer. Pansy in habitual relaxed style came into one lecture with one hand in his pocket and the other holding aloft a jar containing rotting flesh. 'In my hand I hold a syphilised penis'. There was a question from the back row ... 'which hand'.

There were more good looking women doing psychology than economics, so I did a couple of units of psychology. These young ladies were destined to be social workers, deal with drug addicts and in general try to make the world a better place. They certainly made a contribution to my well being.

Spent some time playing billiards and chess. Curiously I would miss lectures because I was in the middle of an interesting chess game, rather than because I was at the pub or had formed a new liason. I did not drink beer which was regarded by the conventional crowd as very odd. Aussies are a conformist lot.

Participated in the intervarsity skiing competition at Thredbo. Picked up 11th spot in the langlauf – it was the right event for a cross country runner. I was in the debating team, the debate I remember was against the 'lifers' in Pentridge the high security gaol about whether Mao was right that 'power came out of the barrel of a gun'. Lots of movies with the Film Society; Italian – La Dolce Vita, French – L'Annee derniere a Marienbad and even some decent stuff from the US – Dr Strangelove. Also 'Battleship Potempkin' and other classics, the still camera with figures falling through the frame is still used. I spent five years at Melbourne University. It still feels more like home than anywhere else I have been.

On graduating, I was booked to go to Europe with some friends. Then a letter arrived telling me that I had been selected for a graduate traineeship (mandarins of the future) with the Commonwealth Public Service Board. The Appointments Board at Melbourne University had assured me that this was the best management training available in Australia at that time. I cancelled the trip to Europe and went to Canberra. Not one of my best decisions.

Twenty First birthday

It was both pathetic and boring. After a few months, I left Canberra and went to work for IBM. So much for the dream of making wise public policy. There is still a need. Contemporary public servants seem to be more interested in their superannuation. An unfunded liability of more than 60 billion dollars. It will be paid for by the productive people in the community. A monstrous theft – much larger than the great train robbery!

The tendency by our public servants to purchase foreign rather than locally produced goods could be regarded as treason. It certainly reduces our capacity to fund their prosperous retirement. These goons don't even understand their own self interest.

Now that we have children who have grown up in Canberra entering the so called 'public service' we can expect their detachment from reality to intensify leading to decisions the are even more foolish. Do you remember the 'recession we had to have'. It wasn't Keating – he was just the Treasury spokesperson. However life continued prosperous for the public servants in Canberra

You have probably heard of IBM. In 1965 they were at the peak of their arc of self importance. They had only recently stopped singing motivational songs each morning. We all wore the white shirt, dark suit uniform and were prohibited from having a glass of wine at lunch. They even insisted that I buy a hat!

Moments after emerging from the hat shop - looking like a real dork at age 22 in suit and hat - a passing truckie exclaimed 'look at that idiot in the hat'. I didn't wear it again.

I know that this sounds like Mao's China with rigidly prescribed codes of dress and behaviour. It was like Mao's China. I didn't get hold of a copy of Mao's little red book until the 70's, but at IBM we had plenty of cliches eg. 'When the going gets tough, the tough get going'. We had branch meetings three mornings a week at eight. Full of pseudo-enthusiastic frenzy and cliche.

I took my secretary out for a farewell lunch when she resigned. We had a glass of red. My IBM boss puffed himself up and said 'now I can sack you anytime I want.' This was my first exposure to the uneducated, ill bred, pushy jerks who flourish like weeds in our poorly tended garden.

I grew up in the shadow of the second world war. My mother lost a brother in the first war and a husband in the second. There was much talk in our family about duty, discipline and honour, the values which have informed behaviour in many parts of the world for millennia. I had read Tolstoy, Ibsen, Shakespeare and Chekov and enjoyed the films of Fellini and the French 'new wave'. Yet here I was in this nest of posturing peasants, in what was supposed to be one of the finest companies in the world!

Honeywell on the other hand were amateurs, the products were OK, but the management was mediocre. You would think in business if you had a better value for money proposition, that you would succeed. Somehow Honeywell rarely succeeded against IBM. IBM wooed the directors and worked down. The well known fear, uncertainty and dread (FUD). Honeywell started with the technology people and worked up. It was clear which approach was more effective.

Beckingsale was a delight. Very bright people making a difference. One colleague had a double first class honours degree in Engineering and Economics from Cambridge. He said that the only thing he recalled from these years was the Engineering Professor who intoned 'when a structure fails .... it becomes a mechanism'. Picture bridges collapsing gracefully. Sorry, an engineers joke.

We had a two day professional development session once a quarter with a dinner on the evening of day one. At one of these dinners our almost PhD psychologist was declaiming 'you show me the man who is absolutely certain of anything – and I will show you a fool'! There was a moment of silence while we processed this revelation. Then a colleague asked 'are you absolutely certain of that'? Much mirth followed. There were no more revelations that evening.

I was involved in a takeover study for an agricultural chemicals manufacturer, a logistics study for a plastics machinery manufacturer, a marketing study for a toilet, stove and heater manufacturer, a systems study for a hotel motel chain and some high level recruiting. We took the view that bright people could make a contribution in any environment and we did.

I then freelanced as a management consultant and actor for a couple of years. Picked up some consulting assignments (specification of a management reporting system for Commodore Motels, and a systems recovery assignment for Kingfisher a supermarket hardware manufacturer) and bit parts in the TV soaps of the time - Homicide, Matlock, Divvy 4 and Bellbird. I was the policeman, school teacher, farmer that sort of thing, just a question of getting into character really.

I read Stanislavski and went to a two week drama school given by Hayes Gordon on 'method acting' and actively explored this new world. To understand method acting, picture Marlon Brando mumbling his way through 'The Godfather'.

My last television commercial in 1972 was for TAA who were claiming to be 'a little bit more friendly'. I was the businessman waving goodbye to 200 ecstatic staff on the tarmac. You could not see that I had picked the top off a cold sore on my nose that morning. I imagined that this would be helpful and that they would be able to fill the hole with make-up. That failed, so all the mug shots were from the left.

Meanwhile I was living at La Trobe University as a tutor in Glen College. We studied the John Wayne, John Ford movies and made some of our own. While the John Ford movies work very well as formulaic westerns, there is lots of sophistication buried in them. Have a look for the contribution to the plot by minor characters.

Making movies at La Trobe University

In Europe and America it was common for young adults to leave home and live in or near the University to do some growing. La Trobe tried to get all students, including the commuters extensively involved in the College system. It didn't work. In matriarchal Melbourne these young adults were expected to be home in time for dinner with mum.

I had left home at age 18 and lived in various digs around the university. I spent the summer breaks earning enough money to last through the next year, working as a fruit picker, waiter, factory worker and market researcher. I imagined that one day I might apply the insight gained from these diverse experiences to the making of movies with the broad sweep of Fellini.

During lunch with the fruit pickers one day two Jugoslavs arrived brandishing screwdrivers and threatened to inflict serious damage on a New Zealander. Soon the Jugslavs were running for their lives down the road to the manager's house with an angry mob pursuing them throwing rocks and brandishing iron bars. The dispute had started the previous evening when one or the other had thrown an empty beer bottle across through the roof space into an adjoining cubicle. Interesting to see the rough justice of the mob.

We used to swim against the swimming club in the local town - Shepparton - at the end of the day. Some of my mates were surfers so we won most of the races. You can get some insight into the fruit pickers life from a play called *The Summer of the Seventeenth Doll*. They start picking fruit in Queensland and follow the sun South as the fruit ripens. This happened every season, so the regulars had a girlfriends in many towns. A bit like sailors really.

On Saturdays I would hitch hike to Melbourne, borrow my grandmother's car and take my girlfriend to the movies. This was the girl I should have married. She was calm, wise and lovely. We thought that we knew how to deal with the world. Picture a church group weekend with all the girls sleeping on one side of the living room and all the boys on the other - except for us. One of the preachy guys admonished us with the pronouncement that this was not a spectator sport. The reality was that he fancied the lady in question but was out of luck.

One evening I arrived late for a pennant squash match at the Melbourne Cricket Club. The place was locked and bolted. Now I was captain of the team. It would be poor form to be a 'no show'. How to get in? I had done some rock climbing. I reckoned I could climb up the outside of the stand, over the roof and drop in. So I parked my car under a sign protruding from the edge of the stand, put on my squash gear, stuffed the racquet down the back of my track suit and climbed on top of the car. Grasped the sign and scrambled up onto the wire mesh beside the stairs. You know how it is, the possibility of falling and splattering on the pavement becomes more vivid when you are clinging to the wire mesh half way up. I arrived in time for my squash match, full of adrenalin and played the best squash of my career. Maybe I needed a little more adventure.

At the same time, I was reading the yachty magazines and liked the look of the Drascombe Longboat. Strongly built, spartan, simple, maybe a diminutive cousin of the Viking longboat and the Scottish Coble. I had read Eric the Red's Saga and The Saga of the Greenlanders about the discovery of America in around 1000 AD. Clearly you could do a lot in a strongly built open boat. I ordered one through the mail from Honnor Marine and advised that I would arrive in UK in October to collect it.

One of my friends thought that I might need a spare spar in case the mast broke. He presented me with a rowing oar. In the spirit of this generous contribution I took the oar on the Jumbo jet to England. On arrival in UK, rented a car, strapped the oar to the roof and headed off to pick up my boat at Totnes in Devon.

Donna Elvira

The name was to be Donna Elvira. If you know your opera, Donna Elvira takes a lot of punishment and comes back for more. Just what you would want from a boat. Proud, strong, purposeful, and she could sing!

I met the designer of the boat, David Watkinson. He had designed a strong and seaworthy yacht, suitable for sail training or open boat adventures. Ken Duxbury had already done some Mediterranean cruising in a Drascombe lugger. I intended to do something similar in the Greek islands.

Donna Elvira was 21ft 9 inches long and about six feet wide. A large rowing boat with two masts and brown sails. A 212 pound iron centre board and an iron rudder provided some stability. The main sail was loose footed and gunter rigged – in plain speak, there was no wooden spar at the base of the main sail, however there was a wooden extension reaching up beyond the top of the mast. I could raise or lower the mast without assistance. I had a block and tackle and some inflatable rollers so that I could pull the boat up onto the beach without assistance. The hull was fibreglass in a clinker style. A bit spartan, but strong and seaworthy. Check the cover for more details on the boat or go to

http://www.drascombe-association.org.uk/drascombe.htm

I purchased a flagon of rough cider for the launching ceremony. English damsel intoned 'may god bless this vessel and all who sail in her' and whacked the scrumpy flagon onto the stem head. She objected to the use of this offensive word God, but I insisted. The flagon didn't break, it slipped from her hand and smashed on the concrete. Did this mean that I should abandon the voyage or the damsel?

First, we should test the boat. Went for a short trial sail in the river Teign. As we returned someone shouted 'pull out the rudder', I lifted it out. The boat is now out of control and hits the concrete dock. We are not starting well. Paddled round the corner, tied the boat up and went to dinner. When I came back the boat was hanging ten feet in the air by its mooring lines. Where I come from the tide rises and falls a few feet. Here in the river Teign it was 15 feet. How was I supposed to know that?

Enough problems for one day. I lowered the boat into the water, clambered in and slept.

Donald Crowhurst had left from Teignmouth on his ill fated solo voyage in the 'round the world' race. The locals were a little concerned that they might be host to another yachtie headed for trouble. Don't know if this has some cosmic significance, but my boat ended up in Kingston Jamaica where Crowhurst's boat came to rest. I am a lot more sympathetic to Crowhurst than the two journalists who wrote the book about him. Unless you have spent a couple of months on your own at sea it is difficult to understand how things change. The conventional, conformist, 'what will the neighbours think' mode where most people spend their lives falls away. So the mind can roam unconstrained. Is this crazy. Well probably. Sanity is defined as doing the conventional things. The pervasive virtual lobotomy.

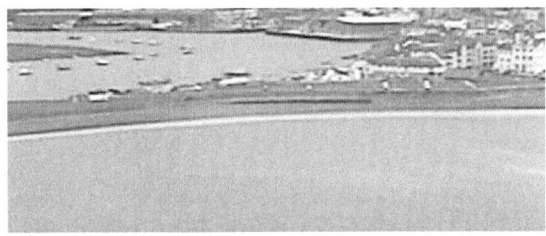

River Teign – where we christened Donna

The wind was blowing strongly onshore and the locals were not going out. I tried sailing against it for half a day, but made no progress. There were some exciting moments getting back through the shore break and up the river. I would face the large waves, get over them and then turn and run for the shore until some more large waves came. I had been in surf boats in Australia so I had some idea how to deal with the surf. Didn't seem to know too much about sailing however.

Next day we put Donna on the trailer and drove up the coast to Newhaven and dropped her in the river. Very grateful for the help of Malcolm the foreman from Honnor Marine. I headed up the river and spent my first night at anchor. Donna was a very light boat and every breath of wind pushed her this way and that. You know how it is with first time experiences, you are on full alert in case there are problems you have not understood. Woke frequently to check that everything was in order. Tide went down a long way and left me in a deep trench. However I was not aground, so grabbed a little more sleep.

Watched pairs of swans flying up river to their nesting place. Wondered if I might ever be part of a pair. I had known some wonderful women. Somehow never got to the altar. A couple of near misses, but they don't count, do they? I had been at Melbourne University not long after Germaine Greer and Barry Humphries. The traditional certainties about relationships were being mocked. This was the era of unisex dressing, burning of bras and casual liason. Here I am alone in my boat - probably not going to solve that problem this evening.

Next morning raised the mast and headed back down the river. As we approached the bridge, realised that it would have been better to get under the bridge and then raise the mast. Will we make it? Turned to head back up the river, but the current was too strong. Executed a pirouette of doubt as I went under the bridge backwards. Out into the grey English Channel. Raised the sails and ghosted towards Dover. Spent most of the day off the white cliffs making very little progress and headed back into the harbour at Newhaven. What was it about Bruce and the spider?

Met Gary Griffin a professional yacht delivery skipper. He was leaving that evening to deliver a Contessa 26 to Ramsgate, would I come? Of course. We had a brisk sail up the Channel with spinnaker up most of the way. We surged past a pier at midnight where the new owner was standing. A little added value to show the owner how well his new yacht performed. Gary made the Channel seem very civilised.

Had a few drinks and a chat with John the harbour master. This led me to consider putting Donna on the ferry to France. It was late in the season, the channel can be ugly and I didn't know my boat very well. However it cost fifty quid. So I spent the next few days sailing in light winds to Folkstone. Amazed how many Poms were fishing instead of working.

Spent a night in a lodging house at Folkstone so that I could have a shower and get some proper sleep. I had been awake for a couple of days. This was the beginning of a convention whereby one should enjoy the pleasures of the port before sailing. I think that this convention goes back some thousands of years.

Next morning headed across the Channel towards Calais. Lots of shipping about. Light winds. Sailing with main sail only. Should have had the jib up, but didn't know if I would be able to get it down while I was at sea and was worried about capsize. Saw a light ship, but couldn't work out if it was Varne or South Goodwin. The current is very strong here, so I was probably going sideways faster than forwards. Looking back, I could have used the outboard and crossed in about five hours instead of eighteen.

Spent the day dodging ships and making slow progress across the channel. The British plum on the BBC warned of ' ... possible gales later'. It got dark. Didn't know where I was. Motored up to the biggest light I could see, thought that it might be the Dyck light vessel. Asked 'where am I'. He said 'ici Sandettie'. It was the Sandettie light ship.

A very gracious French travailleur took me on board gave me a couple of scotches and showed me on the chart the way to Calais. He gave me the bearings for three marks. Here I am in the middle of the English Channel at nine PM. What I would have liked to do was spend the night on the light ship. This was clearly not an available option. I started the outboard motor and departed into the night.

The first two marks appeared exactly where expected. Missed the third one by a large margin. I suspect that the tide changed and washed me in the other direction. Smelt the sewage and detected the beach - I had a choice, turn left or right. I turned right. Some time later I saw some harbour entrance lights. But they were back to front.

I am feeling a little weary as it is after two AM in the morning. How can the entrance lights be back to front? As I got closer I could see the two long piers extending from the entrance to the port. I was close to the beach and looking out to sea. This is why the lights appeared to be back to front, I was looking at them from the 'land side' rather than the 'sea side'. Motored out past the end of the piers and almost collided with a Polish yacht heading out without lights. So close to the safety of the harbour and almost sunk.

Entrance to Calais harbour

This was the first time I had entered a foreign port. Am looking up from my little boat to the dock expecting to see lots of customs and immigration officials. I scanned the dock from end to end. There was no one in sight. What do I do now? I clambered up onto the dock and looked around. Can't clear customs if there is no one here. Tomorrow I will sort out the paper work and get my *permis* to use the canals. Tied up to a buoy and slept.

The yachties introduced me to Stanislav Chisek who was heading my way in a small yacht - Narcyz. He was Polish and had official approval to make a voyage from Poland to East Germany. He ended up in Venezuela.

It was October, a bit late in the season, but I wanted to get down to the Mediterranean. I had read several books on traversing the French canals. Now I would see what it was really like.

French Canals

Travelling through France in the canals is a elysian or is it bucolic experience. Maybe both. This is a dream world where everything happens slowly much of it pleasurable. I would be up at five most mornings, searching for a boulangerie. A fresh pain chocolat or two to start the day. Not quite a James Bond breakfast, but very toothsome.

Barge in lock – you don't want to collide with one of these

The French canals had lots of commercial traffic. Chalombiers spent their lives on the barges and delivered the heavy stuff – sand and gravel - all around France. Their kids used to grow up on the barge and be inducted into the profession. Then the government required the kids to be sent to school. Strangely when the kids discovered life beyond the barge they did not want to come back. The chalombier profession was dying out.

There was lots of tourist traffic too. It was much safer to go down the French canals to the Mediterranean, rather than round the Atlantic coast and across the stormy Bay of Biscay. I fell into conversation with an American family. Orthodontist with wife and daughter. They had set sail and learned navigation on their way across the Atlantic. Loyal, patriotic and diplomatic, he answered my praise of the French baguette with some words about the American bread lasting longer. True enough, but who cares - tomorrow I can have another fresh baguette.

The fog rolled in near Cambrai. The rules are that everything must stop in the fog. Picture this, I have been on the boat for two weeks, have not shaved or showered and am dressed in an old military greatcoat. In this fashion I began visiting the jewellery shops of Cambrai to see if they were interested in Australian opals. Some Aussies think that opals are unlucky, doesn't seem to bother the French. The jeweller wanted to make a setting with an opal centrepiece and a row of diamonds around the border. The cost of the opal was incidental for him. We did a deal.

I had bought these opals duty free and wholesale so there was a small margin. For a moment I imagined that my strategy of taking opals rather than travellers cheques was a winner. How boring are travellers cheques! Didn't manage to convert any more opals until Barbados. People now tell me that unauthorised trading can lead to the seizure of the boat by the authorities. That would not have been convenient.

Donna in lock – note big gates in the foreground, close the gates fill the lock with water and Donna floats up to the level of the next section of the canal

Lots of barges queued up waiting for the lock to open when the fog cleared. As a pleasure craft I would have to wait till all the commercial craft went through the lock before I got my turn. Seemed to me this might be a very long time. Went and had a chat to the lock keeper in my broken French. Soon the first set of four barges entered the lock. The lockkeeper then closed one gate so that I could zap in and lie transverse across the stern of the barges. He then closed the other gate and we were floated up with the first group of barges to the higher level of the next section of canal. That saved more than a day.

The canals were closed on Armistice day so I hitched to Paris. Viewed the Tour Eiffel, Arc de Triomphe, Notre Dame and the Champs Elysee. Spent the night with a delightful Australian couple, plus three kids and a nephew on their boat in the Seine. He had been an actuary with AMP in Sydney, surname perhaps 'Hardy'. They had taken nine months off and were having a great time exploring France by boat. Got a ride back with a French guy in a VW. He told me about the 100 plus people killed on French roads each weekend as he drove like a man possessed through pouring rain.

Early beard and spiked hair

Met some English who mocked the Arc de Triomphe because it did not have Waterloo listed. Much later I find out that Wellington commanded 107,000 troops out of a total of 250,000 and tens of thousands of these were from European countries. Brits should check the role of the 'Grand old Duke of York' in obstructing Wellington's efforts to raise and provision an adequate force.

Blucher on the other hand had four corps each of 30,00 men who had been trained by General Gerhard Von Scharnhorst who also trained Karl Von Causewitz. Wellington correctly described his victory as a 'damned near-run thing'. William Siborne's jingoistic 'history' has been discredited. Sadly this is the version the informs the view of most Brits.

Ask anyone who knows some Scottish history about Darien. The Scots in 1698 gathered every available investment dollar in Scotland and set up a colony at Darien on the isthmus between North and South America. Their intention was to tranship goods from the Pacific to the Atlantic and bypass the voyage around Cape Horn. A great idea which could have produced a prosperous and independent Scotland. The Scots were unable to trade with Europe at this time because of an English blockade. Some bad decisions, some bad luck, a feverish climate, both Spanish and English hostility and the expedition failed.

The Scots had another chance with North Sea oil. Some would say that under the treaty of 1707 this resource belonged to the Scots. No deal. The English standard of living was propped up by North Sea oil for decades. The 'Speccie' reports that finally in the Blair cabinet, the Scots are having their say. About time.

Are we there yet?

While many English people one meets are delightful, the decisions at the National level are very hard headed. America too knows how to pursue its own self interest as reported by Kissinger in *Diplomacy*. In stark contrast, no one in Australia has bothered to define the national interest. Therefore we can't pursue it. We just tag along behind whoever is the toughest guy in the playground.

A French architect in Joinville recommended a night club. We had a great time. He was disappointed that he didn't make out with the Aussie blonde. Strange how blokes so often target the bubbly blonde. There are usually better options available, ask Jane Russell.

Met Dick (oral surgeon from Kansas City) and family on Alano, Derek on Je Reviens and John on Maylo. We travelled in convoy out of the canal and into the flooding Saone. Some of the locks were closed as the river up so high that it was flowing over the top of the barrage. I had to decide early because the river was flowing faster than Donna could travel. Get it wrong and you go over the waterfall. Not a good idea.

Met Peter Crozier and Jean (Aussie teachers) on Nike at Macon and travelled with them down to the Yacht Club du Rhone. We had some confusion with the locals when Pete was trying to say that he would prefer not to be bitten on the leg by the Alsation. How is your French, 'jambe and jambon' sound pretty similar. Translates into 'leg or lolly'. Isn't English the Lingua Franca.

Entering lock – gates close and you are floated up to the next level

The next stop was Lyons with more than 50 boats tied up five to ten deep. I almost collided with a barge when a tree branch became entangled in my outboard and I couldn't change the direction of the boat. A Brit got stuck transverse across the upstream side of a bridge pylon. The flooding river was crushing the boat against the pylon. He was lucky to get off without losing his boat.

We were all discussing the flood running at about eight knots through Lyons and considering if we would continue. I wanted to get down to the Med so I departed next morning at 0905 ahead of the crowd.

One evening I turned in towards the dock at Tournon to stop for the night. I am pointing upstream doing four knots the current is running eight knots and backwards I went down the river. No big thing you might say, pull in at the next dock. However it was getting dark. I consulted the canal pilot book. Three kilometres down the river the canal branched off the river to the left into La Roche du Glun. As long as I made it into the canal I would be all right. I kept to the left and strained my eyes into the darkness. Marked off the navigation posts in my canal chart as I passed them. Should be soon. Ah, there it is. Went up the canal a short way and tied up for the night.

Went to the local village to post some letters. When I was away from the boat, I worried about both thieves and rats. Perhaps they have some characteristics in common. One night while cooking dinner - tied up to the edge of a canal - a large rat leapt aboard and landed on my forearm. A reflex flick of the arm and he was flying through the air. I then anchored in the middle of the canal for the night. While these rats could swim, they had trouble clambering onto the boat.

Paused alongside a Dutch boat in sight of the Pont D'Avignon. Well the remaining third of the Pont D'Avignon. The Dutch 30 something couple were calm, cool, happy and relaxed in the way of the 70's. They shared their lunch of fried potatoes and bacon with me. I didn't know about the munchies or that hemp had been a popular crop in the Netherlands for centuries. These guys had stepped out of the conventional world and were wandering around in their yacht untouched by the hypocrisy and flatulence of mainstream life.

Down towards the mouth of the Rhone I was making great time in the flooding river. However I still had to stop at night. One night it got later and later and I didn't get to a town or dock (1645 hours at K303). It was getting very dark. Maybe I should put out the anchor.

Now I was in a flooding river, very wide, all the surrounding country flooded. Didn't want to hook my anchor on a fence. Nor did I want the anchor to drag in the night and get me into trouble. Headed out of the main channel towards the trees. Dropped the pick and swung there. Lots of branches and other rubbish coming down the river and scratching past Donna. However we seemed to be OK, so I slept. Tomorrow would be Marseille.

Marseille has been in operation for thousands of years. It was at one time a Phoenician trading port. I suspect that the Neanderthals were here for a long time before that. The fishermen still head out each evening. Late each morning they come back to the dock in the main port and sell their catch direct to the public. No middlemen or tax officials stealing the profits here.

My outboard had been sputtering and dying out. Unfastened it and carried it to the local dealer one Francis Dicorato looking for a warranty fix. This was a small nautical shop with five staff. The only one who did any work was the 17 year old apprentice. He pulled my engine to pieces and put it together again. How do I know. I came each day and watched. Still seemed to sputter as it had when I brought it in. Francis expected to be paid for this ineffective work. He wasn't. Later took it to England and had it properly fixed under warranty. It is the people who 'do stuff' in Britain who deserve the bouquets.

Breakfast in Marseille was a Grand Flute and a lump of Emmental cheese eaten while wandering the streets. Roamed all over this wonderful old town. However it was time to move on. I headed round towards St Tropez. Paused at Les Iles D'Heyeres. On one of these islands the convention was that at the moment of disembarkation from the ferry all passengers must remove all clothes. A fresh and natural approach.

I hitched round towards St Tropez to collect mail. Late in the day I caught up with a hippy couple with a broken down 'deux chevaux'. I suspected that it was a blocked carburettor. Swapped the leads to the two end spark plugs, gave it a rev and cleared the blockage. He was an artist in carved leather and she was a painter. They gave me a lift, dinner and bed for the night. The dinner was some strange looking mushrooms. I was trying to politely decline.

She was offended by my lack of trust. Eventually ate the mushrooms. Tasted OK and I slept well.

Continued on to St Tropez walking through most of the day. Passed Port Grimaud – one of the first holiday developments where you could have the beemer at the front door and the yacht in the canal at the back. Had a beer in the Plaza. This was 12 December. The bikinis had all gone home. Arranged to have the boat taken to a storage yard for winter, grasped the outboard and took the train to London. Next summer I would continue on my way to the Greek islands.

Alain Bombard - advice

When I met Alain Bombard in 1973, he was Director of a marine research institute working on issues like cleaning up the Mediterranean. There were floating islands of plastic garbage and much else that needed to be addressed.

Alain Bombard

In 1952 he made a voyage across the Atlantic from the Canaries to Barbados in a rubber raft taking neither food nor water. His mission was to demonstrate that shipwrecked people die of panic rather than necessity. His book 'Nauffragé Volontaire' - shipwrecked voluntarily - records the experience.

He told me that there were three things to know about the Atlantic. Firstly, in a small boat when you shoot the sun with your sextant it is easy to mistake the top of a wave for the horizon and get the wrong answer. His notion was that you should count the waves so that you knew when you were on a large one, should be every seventh. Later I got the knack of shooting the sun. Seemed to me that you could see the dark line of the horizon and differentiate it from the nearest big wave. I got it right most days.

When you are shooting the sun every day it is clear when one shot is out of sequence. However if you miss a few days as I did close to Barbados, it can increase the level of tension. I was doing a Columbus style crossing getting on the Latitude of Barbados and running along that Latitude until I hit the target. You can see that if you can't shoot the sun for a few days, you can easily miss an island 26 miles long.

The sextant is a device with angled mirrors and filters so that you can look at the sun and the horizon at the same time. You wind the knob until the sun looks as if it is sitting on the horizon. You can then read the angle which shows how high the sun is in the sky. You need the angle of the sun at its highest point, so you take a number of shots until the angle starts to decline. You then extract some numbers from the nautical tables, do some sums and you have your latitude. My sextant was an Ebbco plastic one which cost fifteen English pounds. It had a large index error, but otherwise seemed to work all right. Still does. I recently used it to observe the transit of Venus.

The second thought from Bombard was that when you do not know your longitude (how far you have gone) then you can get depressed. Sure enough. I would check all around the boat each morning in case by some freak circumstance I was still within sight of Africa. After 50 days at sea I had no idea how far I had come, or how far there was to go. I ended up doubting the calculations I used to process the daily sextant sun shot and everything else. So I went back to fundamental geometry and proved to myself that the sums worked. Did that make me feel better? Not much.

However at the practical level it did not matter whether I knew exactly where I was. The only strategy that made any sense was to get as far West as I could each day. Life is very straightforward on the ocean. Stay afloat and keep heading in the right direction.

Bombard's third point was that when you are becalmed you become the centre of an eco system. Fish use the boat as a reference point. Then the sharks come to eat the fish. Seemed to me that the sharks were eating my lunch. So I prodded them in the back with my trident. No reaction. Sharks have no sensory nerves in the skin. So I went for the eyes. Even the tiny brain of the shark could work out that this was a hostile environment and they retreated. In the 'Old Man and the Sea', Santiago rammed his harpoon into the sharks brain. I would like to have had a whalers lance or a rifle so that I could have done the same.

In Barbados I met someone whose father was present when Bombard landed. He reported that Bombard was not in very good condition red spots all over him. However he made a very courageous voyage and proved his point - I salute him.

Mediterranean Coast of France and Spain

Got a contract programmers job in London for a few months, then spent Easter in Scotland with friends. I stayed with the Chairman of the Glacier Metal Corporation a company that was very innovative in both technology and human relations. I bought and read the books by Elliot Jacques prior to the Easter visit so I would know the background. Original thinking about the impact of the time span between making a decision and knowledge of outcome, and some great tribology technology. Tribology not one of your words? It is the science of things rubbing together. No, not romance, science. Picture teflon style bearings in cars. The car makers of the time were slow to adopt this technology, preferring to stick with the well known ball bearings.

Learning to play the bagpipes in Saint Andrews, Scotland

Bought a kilt and some bagpipes. Hitchhiked from Saint Andrews to Marseille in my kilt. The last car off the ferry in Boulogne was a Truimph Vitesse. Fortunately, he gave me a lift. A Brit who was on his way to Law School in Switzerland. We stayed overnight in Paris with his lady friend. I slept on the floor in the kitchen. By the time I had bought him lunch, it would have been cheaper to catch the train.

In Lyon some ten year old kids were humming 'Scotland the brave' when they saw me in my kilt - shades of the Auld Alliance. I gave them each a turn on the bagpipes. A van stopped to give me a lift. It was some hippies going to a rock concert. French rock didn't have the urgency, energy, anarchy and anger of the Anglo Saxon stuff. However these were pleasant people trying to find their way in our expedient and cynical world.

Then, got the boat out of storage, trailed it back to the coast and launched. Now you may recall that I was planning to island hop around Greece seeking the intrigue and mystery described in The Magus by John Fowles. Identity games with identical twin sisters and an ageing Greek ringmaster.

On the other hand I had been reading about the Fairfax adventure rowing across the Atlantic. He crossed from the Canaries to Florida in a purpose built 30 ft rowing boat. I reckon that the high structure turned it into an inefficient yacht. He took a very long time to cross.

Seemed to me if he could row across the Atlantic I should be able to sail across. In fact two longshoremen had rowed across the Atlantic in 1898. Lots of people made the southern crossing from the Canaries to Barbados, including Columbus. Why not me. I might even make it to Australia. I turned right and headed for Gibraltar.

A ships captain warned me about the Mistral. On a fine day with a clear blue sky you can suddenly be knocked flat by stronger than gale force winds. The cold air from the Alps funnels down the Rhone valley and out to sea (can be force 11). I reckon that it was a Mistral that dismasted Nelson's ship when he was stalking Napoleon in 1798.

I didn't get a Mistral, but there was more wind than I was accustomed to. Took a lot more water on board than I had expected. My lovely fresh baguettes were soaked in sea water. This was not satisfactory.

Tied up in the river at Saint Marie de La Mer during the annual festival of gypsies. Can you imagine thousands of gypsies converging on one place for a festival. Had many offers to have my palm read and my money blessed. My thought was that anything not nailed down would disappear from my boat the moment I was out of sight. I hurried back to the boat and sailed on seeking any town which did not have a festival of gypsies.

Arrived in Sete. It was full of short, dark, swarthy, piratical looking men. There are lakes in behind Sete where the pirates used to hide. I went into these lakes and tied up at Marseillan. A delightful little town with a yacht basin and a town square full of boule playing locals. This is where Noilly Prat is made. I pulled the boat out of the water so that I could paint the bottom and build a structure to keep the waves away from my baguette. No gypsies in sight.

I walked the two kilometres to the next town Agde and bought a couple of sheets of 19mm marine ply and carried them back to the boat. Then I built a locker in the mid section of the boat. Sealed it watertight with lots of fibreglass. It was two feet deep three feet wide and seven feet long. I planned to stow my gear in one side and sleep on the other. That should keep the baguettes dry.

Agde was a Greek outpost of the City of Marseille some 2,500 years ago and still has a statue of Aphrodite. These days there are many aspirant aphrodites on the beach at Cap d'Agde.

I meet a young Frenchman with a duckling. George and I hit the beach. He is followed along the beach by this tiny duckling. This generated a number of conversations with young ladies. It is an approach I hadn't seen before. Aphrodite meets duck. Seemed to be effective.

A group of us were playing guitar and singing towards midnight in Agde when the police arrived and sent us home. I make a comment to George about living in a police state. He wanted to prove how free people are in France, and began shouting anti government political slogans. Good thing the police had gone.

Some teenagers skipped school and came swimming and diving off the bridge with me in the river Herault. They told me about the desire for Occitanéé to separate from the rest of France. We are in Languedoc – the land of Oc where they speak the in the tongue of Oc. *Occitanéé Libre!*

On down the coast to La Nouvelle. I walked to the end of the pier and looked along the coast where I was planning to go next day. Fell into conversation with Kerstin Johansson from Gothenburg. We picnicked by the canal and chatted about many things. It was wonderful. My log records that I 'ached like 19 year old, full of passion'.

My friends advise that this is not great poetry, however it is what I wrote at the time and attempts to express my feelings.

Endure I shall

Northern love
When will we meet
To satisfy our longing

I need you now
And every hour
My heart to you belonging

This ocean seeks
to keep me here
forever sailing West

Forty and seven
days I've sailed
A long endurance test

Endure I shall
For now I want
My life with you to share

> Growing stronger
> Every day
> Knowing that we care
>
> The gods decreed
> That we should meet
> And we shall meet again
>
> Travelling then
> Down life's long road
> Nothing twixt us twain.

Kerstin quoted her grandmother as saying the best thing about a holiday is to depart with a thousand crowns and return with nine hundred. You will have to get a Swede to explain this to you. I suspect that it is something to do with fine upright Scandinavians not being ripped off by thieving Southern Europeans. When Kerstin headed back for Gothenburg, I wanted to go too.

Next day I continued along the coast. The wind was very strong. I had never sailed in this much wind before so I kept near to the beach in a few feet of water so that I could jump out if necessary. This will seem silly to experienced yachtsmen. However it was a strong offshore breeze and I was frightened of being blown out to sea.

I downed the sails and motored into the very next harbour, the tiny Rocher de St Pierre. Spent a pleasant afternoon chatting to some medical students. These students in their dad's 26 ft yacht headed out into the strong wind well ahead of me. The French have a delightful 'devil may care' attitude.

Later I followed them to Port Vendres the last harbour on the French coast before you get to Spain. A secure little bolt hole. A pleasant lunch, a night of partying and off around the corner to Spain. My love of things French has lingered.

In Cadaques I met a young Oxbridge type Charles who had come down to learn painting from Salvador Dali in Port Ligat. He ended up taking lessons from a pupil of the master rather than the master himself. His speciality was doorways. Every day I would see him sketching outside some doorway. Think he was hoping to fall into conversation with one of the lovelies emerging from the doorway. Ducks and doorways, clearly I needed to develop a fresh approach to romance.

I played chess outside the Bar Maritim in Cadaques, bypasses the language barrier, but didn't help in the romance department. Met a German Schoolteacher with his wife and two young blokes Gerard, Margaret, Dedlef and Haiko. We all went out to dinner. The Sangria and the conversation were outstanding. They talked about how the Germans worked hard and made some of the finest products in the world. They were proud of their country and interested in mine. We did not talk about the war.

Later discovered that the guy who ran the local night club was an Aussie. We drank and chatted till four in the morning. Then I stumbled down to the beach to look for my boat.

The dingy had gone. My boat was anchored in the middle of the harbour. I did - as you would have done - took my clothes off and began swimming around the harbour looking for it. I was criss-crossing the harbour for a long time before I found it. Rowed it into the shore and picked up my clothes. Back out to the middle of the harbour for some sleep. I was beginning to like Spain.

Next day the wind was fair so I departed at eight. Tummy was feeling a bit funny. Spent five hours vomiting over the side, but made some distance down the coast. I could barely walk when I went ashore that evening at Estartit. I had passed lots of cruise boats full of English singing loudly 'maybe its because I'm a Londoner that I love London town'. The English working class on holiday are not a pretty sight. Local establishments were tuned to this clientele with signs like 'Fish and Chips spoken here'.

Further down the coast came into Barcelona at two in the morning. The fishing fleet was going out. I had no lights so I was dodging about a bit. Tied up and climbed up to the dock. Saw a green uniform guardia civil with three cornered hat. He ran in the other direction.

You don't expect the guy with the gun to do the running. I confess that I probably looked a bit scrappy, surely not that bad. Maybe it was the military great coat and the big red beard triggering some deep memory of Viking invaders.

Spent some very pleasant days in Tarragona with six Californians. They had surfed in Hawaii and Australia and now being too old for surfing were taking to sailing. Their boat was one of the original 'J' Class yachts used in the Americas Cup before the second world war. Perhaps the *Cambria*. A superb craft which slept 20 and had a 15 foot keel. They were getting the mast shortened. It was cheaper in Spain, although there did seem to be some issues about the quality of the job.

They had a couple of hassles with the Spanish police. On Christmas Eve the police came on board at 11 PM and sent all those of Spanish nationality home. One morning early when two girls were leaving the yacht, the police came running down the dock to enquire if they were Spanish girls. Concern ceased on the discovery that the girls were Austrian. The police were only responsible for the honour and virtue of Spanish women! Let me tell you, this boat was a chick magnet.

J Class

Crossed from Tarragona to Majorca. Took two days, my first overnight sail. Well, I slept most of the first night, there was no wind. Ghosted my way into Pollensa at 2AM the second night. I didn't have any charts, but followed the leading lights into a brand new marina. Probably wouldn't have been on the chart anyway. In the morning I discovered that the leading lights were actually street lights! Seemed to work OK.

Headed off along an ancient winding narrow road with rock wall on each side in search of a supermarket. This was the real Spain very hot sun, dust and many women in black dresses working rather than preening. In Alcudia, noticed the Museo Archeologico de Majorque, and went in. This was where the offspring of the FFV (first families of Virginia) were sent in summer so that the parents would not have to see them then either. I was invited by Professor Dan Woods to sit in on the Archaeology and Spanish course.

The Summer School team – Dan is third from the left

Dan was a truly splendid man who had done a great deal for archaeology in Spain and who was a source of inspiration and delight to his students. We explored a Roman theatre, the remains of the Roman town and circular towers built by the pre Roman Talyots.

Dr Steve Kopper and Chris

The students were very pleasant 20 somethings having a great time in Spain. Am about to list some names. If you know any of these people ask them to get in touch with me. Dave, Tony, Michael, Scott, Brett, Bitsy, Shelton, Christine, John, Lesley

(Boston), Baldy, Murf, Joanne, Jason, Betty (Texas), Barbara, Pat, Irene, Sally, Hilary, and Lyn. Most of them are in the photo above.

Went caving with Dr Steve Kopper, the archaeology lecturer. We climbed down 100 feet into this cave formed during the Wurm glaciation. Then let ourselves down another 50 feet on ropes. A narrow slit where the rocks had been forced apart by the ice. I worried that they might come back together and we would be squished.

Dropping in

Observed the cave spiders waiting for dinner. These guys seldom get fed, so they slow down their metabolic rate and wait. They have enough energy for one run. So they wait for a moth or insect to fall into the cave and then go for it. Miss dinner and you're dead.

We found some ancient myotragus (goat) teeth, rabbit and human teeth, pottery from 3000 BC and the copper part of a dagger sheath. We took a sample of the sediment for paleomagnetic dating. The moment of crisis was when the light went out. Fortunately Steve and Chris had packed spare batteries. However the anxiety climbs as you fumble with the batteries in complete darkness. I reckon we could probably have climbed out in the dark, but the chance of a fall would have been much greater. As with all environments, the quality of the preparation has a huge influence on the outcome.

Steve had been a geologist with an oil company, racing car driver, curator of a museum in the mid-west and was now was completing a PhD in anthropology. Our conversations ranged across a very wide space. Where are you Steve?

We explored a Greek style amphitheatre built by the Romans on the edge of Pollensa, collected shards of Roman pottery and the occasional coin. The Talyots of circular burial chamber fame, would paddle out on rafts and attack passing shipping – this is around the time of Christ. They found as have many others that it was not smart to attack the Romans.

Underground chat

Spent a couple of days in Deja with Steve. Deja is an English enclave on the North coast of Majorca, well away from the tourist throng. Robert Graves had a house there. I joined in the Tuesday chess games on the beach. One local had the members of a Danish squeezebox band as houseguests. We all went to a very long and very serious - twelve tone music - concert. I was delighted to be in an expatriate enclave where most people knew one another and life was particularly civilised.

Very light winds from Majorca to Ibiza. It took three days to go 45 miles. Then a brisk reach across the 60 miles to Denia on the Spanish coast. Thirteen hours at the tiller. At 1AM I was entering Denia harbour. I could not stay awake. Splashed water on my face, gave myself a slap - nothing worked - so I dropped the pick in the harbour entrance and slept.

Ran across Tony Brown a farmer from the Lake District in UK with his wife and ten year old son on Mystico. They were headed for the Pacific via the Straits of Magellan. Let me know if you have heard of their voyage.

As I sailed into Altea a friendly hand was waved to invite me to tie up alongside. Met a happy, friendly, inebriated German couple and their friends. We all went to lunch. They had been trying to have a child for eight years. Eventually they gave up and went sailing. She was pregnant within a few months. Girls you should stress less, that is if you want to breed.

And so it went on down the Spanish coast Alicante, Aguilas, Cartagena, Almeria, Rocketas, Adra, Motril, and Jose Benos with holidaymakers everywhere. Sailed through a sea of condoms and fresh excrement. Many hotels were new and the sewage treatment plant had not been connected. Not much wind so I was into nearly every harbour all the way along the coast from Marseille to Gibraltar. Was touched by the English Lady who said that she did not think that I would get across the Atlantic, I was 'too normal'.

One afternoon I headed for the beach about four miles East of Adra. Anchored in close. A group of ten year old kids appeared and wanted to know if I wanted food, water or oil. Interesting how straightforward, practical and helpful these kids were. The Spanish Policeman appeared, I signalled that I was coming ashore, he wagged his finger and said 'no es possible'.

An uncle of the kids - Paco - paddled out on an inflatable mattress and said 'I hear that you are short of food'. Not really say I, just wanted to do some shopping. Paco told me that the cop was worried that I might be smuggling cigarettes. Later he paddles back out with a couple of bottles of beer. We had a drink together and chatted about Australia. The kindness of strangers.

As I came past the Rock of Gibraltar the water was swirling in ominous ways. I was relieved to find that Donna skimmed across the top of this. Recent investigation has shown that the pillars of Hercules do exist (giant columns mentioned in the bible now underwater) and that there was a major event where the Atlantic broke through and filled the Mediterranean. Could this be the flood recorded in the bible and other ancient stories? Sailed round to the yacht club and dropped the pick.

Now to discover this speck of England at the Southern tip of Spain.

Gibraltar

As the Germans pressed down through Spain during the second world war, the women and children from Gibraltar were evacuated to Madeira. Those left behind, English officers and Spanish maids created a very handsome olive skinned generation. These were called Gibraltarians. They were raised by Spanish grandmothers (both parents working) and so had a prudish Catholic view of life. So I was told.

Destroyer pens in Gibraltar – Donna is the small boat in the middle

Met many wonderful people. A South African who wished to bypass the currency export restrictions built a boat and hid his cache of diamonds in a secret compartment. Then he sailed in the Cape Town – Rio yacht race. After that he continued on to Europe. If the boat sinks you lose everything. He was afloat and happy in Gibraltar.

A South African doctor who treated a Spanish immigrant for exposure. This Spaniard had attempted to migrate to Gibraltar by swimming around the barrier wall. He was being charged with illegal entry and was regarded as a very poor fellow. The doctor enquired why was it so different when he had sailed in on his yacht. This question was not addressed and the Spaniard went to jail.

A couple from Gibraltar who were about to head off across the Atlantic. She was training as a nurse, to deal with medical emergencies while afloat. She was getting used to using words like 'micturition' instead of 'spend a penny' in order to get the nursing ticket. He was planning to drive a wooden plug into the toilet outlet, so that there could be no accident in mid ocean where water got in. He taught navigation. This was where I found out about the four knot current running in through the straits all the time. If you have heard of their voyage please let me know.

With Ed in Gibraltar

Ed and Jenny on Driac II - 25' cutter - presented me with some gymbals to keep my stove level while the boat jumped about. I gave them my guitar, he could play better than me and my outboard, it was useless weight. Preparations were getting serious.

A prior owner of Driac II was a gentleman named MacPherson who in the closing years of his life, 1932-38, logged 45,000 cruising miles. He took his butler. I am told that the butler sailed the boat, cooked the dinner and kept everything in order. I imagined that I had some of the attitudes of the gentleman and certainly had the duties of the butler.

A French friend used to buy his gash from some hippies who lived half way up the rock. One day he arrived to find the police in the middle of a raid. He was taken into custody. This guy had been involved in the 'manifestations' in Paris in 1968. He had the family Chevrolet upside down and burning at the barricades. Did the ructions of 1968 change the world? I don't think so.

They say that you could never have a revolution in Australia. Everyone would want to know which television channel it was on and when it started so they could stay home and watch. We Aussies are committed to apathy.

Police came to the boat that night. They searched the boat and found a bulge in the pocket of my leather jacket.

'What are these.'
'Opals.'
'Did you declare these.'
'No.'
'Think you should.'
Policing in the finest, gracious English style.

I tried to think through all of the things which might go wrong during the crossing. I talked to Ed about medical matters. Peritonitis was his suggestion as an event which is not uncommon and is not easy to deal with alone at sea. Inflammation of the contents of the abdomen. If it is not dealt with you die. The one chance of survival is if the abdomen can be drained and allowed a chance to recover. Ed instructed me to prop myself in a corner, select the pig stabber on my yachtie knife and insert it at the spot marked 'X'. Insert is not the correct term - swing and stab - so that the pain did not stop the action. The 'X' was on the lower left of the abdomen as I recall. What happens next is that you pass out from the pain. With any luck the abdomen drains and you wake up sometime later. Do not try this at home.

Sanding the mast in Gibraltar

Another guy I met took my compasses to the Air Force base for checking. You may not know that compasses need to be regularly checked. I didn't either. Now I had a deviation card for each of my three compasses. I was however hoping to steer by heading for Venus on most nights. Goddess of love – just happened to be lingering over Barbados.

Met an English accountant. He had been dreaming all his life about cruising the Med. Now he was doing it and trying to enjoy himself. He had left it a little late. You must have heard the question 'what do accountants use as a prophylactic? The answer, 'their personality'.

His wife came too. But it wasn't so enjoyable for her. In the home she took most of the decisions. On the yacht he thought he was the boss. Then there was the scrappy crew who shared your living room. The yachtie experience is not everyone's cup of tea.

Delivering stores in Gibraltar – and you thought Donna was small

I did some testing on the sailing characteristics of my boat. Couldn't get her to point higher that 70 degrees off the wind. Means that you could probably get off a lee shore (wind pushing you towards the cliffs). However many boats could point 45 degrees or higher. My boat had a lot more weight in it than it had been designed to carry and I didn't understand much about the importance of the location of anchor points for sails and the slot between headsail and main.

The yacht came with the main sail sheet (rope) attached to a short traveller in the middle of the boat. I had replaced this with two separate main sheets one attached to each gunwale (edge of the boat). You can visualise that the main sail was never trimmed anywhere near the midline of the boat.

Seems obvious when you look back. All I had to do was to tighten both main sheets and I could have positioned the main wherever I liked. Instead I used them one at a time and pointed 70 degrees off the wind.

If I had understood this better I might have ended up in St Lucia rather than Jamaica. Could have spent my days in the Carribean rather than Australia. That would have been more fun, calypso, cooba libra and coffee coloured children.

I had my boat loaded up with bully beef, biscuits, tins of oats and some fresh fruit. I was eating ice cream every day as it would be a while before I could get my next one. I had varnished all the wooden bits and I was ready to go.

On my first three attempts to get out of the straits, the wind dropped out and I had to return. The boys of *Forces Radio* could see all this happening and kept the world informed. You didn't know that the forces had their own radio station? Sure did and it was good.

What do you do after three attempts have come to nothing. You wait for the right wind and have another go.

Down to the Canaries

Did you know that there is a four knot current flowing in through the Straits of Gibraltar all day every day? Not enough water in the rivers which flow into the Mediterranean to replace the evaporation. The Med is getting saltier and saltier. The Baltic on the other hand has a net outflow, so you float a little higher in the Med.

Little Donna does about four knots. How am I going to get out of the straits and into the Atlantic. Got some advice from the British Navy. They showed me the charts of the flow of currents for the Strait – thank you gentlemen. There is an eddy current going my way in close to the Spanish coast as far as Tarifa. I am in it. We are going well. It is 28 September. Out past Tarifa and headed across the shipping lane towards the Atlantic. Then it gets dark. The wind drops out. The fog rolls in. There are lots of ships.

I am in the middle of a busy shipping lane in pea soup fog with no motor. I light the hurricane lantern. Who would be able to see that. Put up the radar reflector. Lit the Tilley lantern. Much brighter, but it only seemed to bring the fog closer. One oar had a square sail lashed to it. Paddled with the other one. Went round in circles. A deep foghorn sounded. The fog horn got louder .... and louder .... and louder. Couldn't make out the direction. I was poised to take evasive action. I pictured the massive bow of the ship appearing out of the fog ten feet away. The polite words are involuntary defecation. I shat myself in fear.

I changed my underwear and scanned the wall of fog. Surely he can see my radar reflector. Don't know how close he passed, but I didn't feel the bounce from the wake. He would be watchful for other large ships like himself. If he hit me he wouldn't even know. A fourteen inch radar reflector is supposed to produce a clear blip on the radar screen. Let's hope so.

An engineer friend advises that the ship could have been five miles away - in cold weather the sound arcs back to the surface. I hold engineers in very high regard, they know useful stuff. In a world blighted by braying, shallow flakes, it is a privilege to know some people of value. Engineers are a bit like yachties - they are tempered by reality – you get it wrong and the bridge falls down or the yacht runs onto the rocks.

Kept watch all through the night. Already sleep deprived on the first night, will have to try to snatch some sleep tomorrow. The fog cleared at dawn. I set sail out into the Atlantic. This should be a little more exciting than day sailing along the Mediterranean littoral. I had this expectation of long rounded swells and firm following breeze. The reality, not much swell or breeze, however I am making some progress in the right direction. As with so many consummations this first day in the Atlantic was an anti climax.

There is much to learn about the Canaries: polygamy, polyandry, a whistling language, arid moonscapes, towering volcanoes, bustling harbours and fruit exports to the European market. I am headed for Puerto de la Luz on Gran Canaria. This is a refuelling spot for ships and a popular starting point for trans-Atlantic sailors. The shipping volume was down when I was there. Could have had something to do with the doubling of the oil price. I didn't see much polygamy, polyandry or whistling. I plan to go back and have another look.

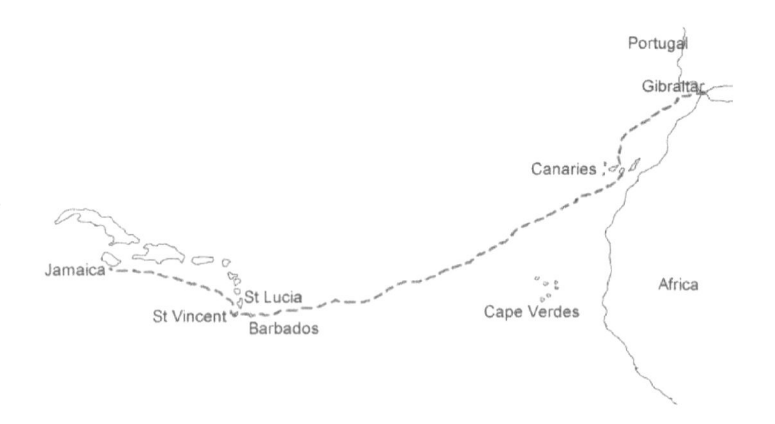

I have ordered a second rudder tiller assembly, some parell beads and other fittings for Donna to be sent there. I plan to have two rudders, one behind the other operating as a giant skeg - like a surfboard – as the square sails pull me across the Atlantic. It is not mentioned in any of the books, but I reckon it can work.

Some people stay close to the coast so that they can run to a harbour if things get ugly. Most yachting accidents happen with people running for harbour in bad conditions. I had met a Swiss naval architect – I know that it sounds unlikely – who had made this voyage in the previous year and had shown me photographs of 30 foot waves with five feet of broken wave surging down the face. His advice was to get out beyond the edge of the continental shelf as soon as possible. I was trying to get 200 miles off the coast where I expected the Atlantic swell to be long and low. It would take a few days. The sea looked OK for now.

Day 3 Got ready for a long, cold, wet night. Three pairs of socks, delicate blue yachty galoshes, track suit pants, slacks, three shirts, two jumpers and leather waistcoat – all covered by an old army greatcoat. Maybe I should have bought some oilskins or a wetsuit top. However, soon I will be in the tropics. Am remembering the Maharaja restaurant in Gibraltar which has the hottest most delicious Chicken Madras ever!

Imagine sitting on fibreglass and holding the tiller 10 hours per day - no wonder my tail was raw

That night I had strong wind. As it strengthens I point Donna into the wind and scramble forward to take in the jib. The sound of the flogging jib was like gunshots. I get the jib down and the sea anchor out. The mizzen on this little boat was reefed by winding the sail around the mast or by pulling the mast out and rotating the mast to get the same effect. I leave only a small rag of mizzen to keep the stern pointing away from the wind. The waves were big, wet and messy. Some came on board. Bailed and sponged to get Donna dry. We seem to be coping with the conditions OK. I have no sense of panic or dread, simply trying to understand what needs to be done and then getting it done.

I was wet and cold, but stayed on deck and tried to snatch some sleep. Two ships passed much too close. I watch the approach and try to decide whether to take the sea anchor in. Don't want to but if I am about to be run down, then I want to get it in quickly and get out of the way.

Towards the end of day five, I looked up to see myself heading across the bows of a freighter. Altered course for him to pass. He seemed to be taking a long time. Then I realised he was closing in for a chat. He was signalling in morse from the bridge. All I knew was that he didn't have anything I wanted except perhaps my position. So I gybed and sailed around his stern and headed off on my 270 heading. He watched for a long time before departing.

Am always happier when there is a ship around if I am moving – then I can get out of his way. I have absolute faith in my capacities. Him......? He is not expecting a toy yacht in the middle of the ocean. He may be on auto pilot and have no one on watch. Even though I am told my radar reflector is big enough to make me look like a battleship - no one may be watching, or they may look out from the bridge and not see what is causing the blip. Always the safest strategy is for me to have control! Also, there are cases of yachts alongside ships rolling in the waves and damaging the crosstrees and mast head fittings. No thank you, I would rather stay away.

Robin Knox Johnson of single handed round the world fame and a ships captain was very disappointed by his fellow merchant captains who kept a poor watch and could have run him down. I had several ships circle me to see if I needed rescuing. Ships are on a tight commercial schedule to deliver their cargo. My boat looked a bit like a lifeboat. It seemed to me very civilised behaviour of these busy ship captains to investigate a small yacht to establish if assistance was required.

Long, gentle, smooth, four foot swell from the North gliding under me. Some cloud all around the horizon. Wonderful silence as the sun slowly raises itself to the horizon. It is so quiet that there seems to be a distant humming buzzz. You would gather from all this writing that the wind is not much good for sailing.

Another ship coming by to check me out. Have just looked up the 'dit dit' I was getting from the signaller on last night's ship. It is 'I' which means I am altering course to port – which is exactly what he was doing. This ship is the 'Mediterranean Sprinter'. Circled me and kept going. Have emptied the bilges, given myself a wash down, and smoked a pipe. Some moments of calm and luxury.

Bombard was right. I have been stationary for a while and there is a school of little fish under me now. They didn't like RyVita or the glinting button off my shirt, so am now offering bully beef. Wish a large Dorado would come, I have a feather lure designed just for him.

Day 6 Waking every half hour through the night to check things out. Wind still light, fog to the North East and a big white light approaching. Usually one can tell that one is not going to be run down as the two masthead lights are separate showing that the ship is on some course that does not involve you. Watched for a little while then could make out the Red on the Port side. Looked as if he might come too close, so I pulled in the sea anchor, inserted rowlocks and lit the Tilley lantern. The hurricane lantern had been burning all along. Before starting to row watched some more. There was only one white light and I could see the Port, but not the Starboard riding light. Reached out for the oars, but as I watched he turned and the sternlight came into view. However I was content. All I ever want at night is to be afloat and well slept in the morning.

Day 7 Rose before dawn, SW wind persists light, but tending to strengthen. Could make 160 and end up in Casablanca. No thank you. Though I would love to visit, the danger of bad weather off there pleases me not. Alternatively, I could make NW which would not terribly useful as I want to go South to the Canaries.

Saw a big black wall of cloud which extended right down to the sea. Tried to work out what it was. Why would there be a wall of cloud? Maybe a warm current meets a cold current and creates this effect. Would it be dangerous? I am ghosting along at one knot surely whatever this is can't be a problem. I enter the cloud and it starts to rain and the wind freshens and changes direction frequently. I spill the wind out of the sails and am OK. What was it? Could it have been caused by the Seine Seamount, where the depth is 32 fathoms compared to the surrounding sea at more than 2000 fathoms? I will be ready next time to collect some water and have a shower. This time it was rather cold and besides I didn't know what was going to happen next.

Too little wind, took down sails and sponged out bilges. Looked for my book on Northern hemisphere astronomy. Couldn't find it, but found others I want to read:
- Robb - Small Boats in Heavy Weather,
- Fairfax – Rowing alone across the Atlantic
- Wells – The History of the World.

String on the upper set of parell beads (these hold the 'gunter' mast extension in place) just broke. Knew it must. Have been trying to buy some for months. Have 12 sets on order from Honnor Marine to be delivered to the Canaries. Fixed the parell beads with a piece of wire scavenged from some dock for emergencies. Am again waiting for wind.

Two weeks already and I am not half way there. However have had good wind for the last 24 hours. Two hours after sundown - lovely wind that would allow me to make three knots. Full moon – beautiful night. Unfortunately must sleep.

Day 15 Three hours before dawn - up again and getting ready to depart wind force 2-3 NNE, small sea. Ship just passing. Funny how they only come during the night. Battery for compass light defunct two days ago. Consigned it to the ocean. Night sailing now involves holding lantern near compass to line up course, then steering by the stars if visible. Too much moon and cloud at the moment.

Another ship before dawn. Think he pulled up to have a chat. Would have run into his side if I hadn't gone about. Another ship, must be in a shipping lane. Later another two ships in sight. Then two more. Hope I can get rid of this traffic jam by sleeping time. The next one is behind me maybe I am moving out of the shipping lane.

Just remembered a can of peaches I brought along for a treat. Am devouring them. Who needs an occasion. Gut didn't like peaches. I will stick to bully beef and biscuits from now on.

Have had a prickling or biting sensation in my sleeping bag every night for months now. Still can't decide if it is prickling or biting. Still I get to sleep so I suppose it doesn't matter that much. Have inspected sleeping bag in detail several times. Could be glass fibres from the locker construction job. Cleared out little stones and grass seeds, but still I get bitten. C'est la vie.

Have been moving at 2-3 knots all day, wonderful to have wind. Have been singing snatches from the Choral movement of Beethoven's Ninth. I do miss good music.

Let's talk about navigation. Traditionally, sextant, chronometer and nautical tables. Get a shot of a couple of stars at twilight do some sums, plot the intersecting lines on the chart and there you are. In the 70's you could get a radio direction finder. I had one. This device gives you the bearing of the radio source – sometimes a beacon sometimes a radio station. Get a couple of those and you are where the lines cross. The moisture in my open boat was not good for the radio direction finder and it ceased operation. Perhaps you can see why I have decided to avoid electrical nick knacks on the next boat.

The next alternative is dead reckoning. Every hour you write down how far you have gone in what direction. Often using a taffrail log which indicates how far you have gone through the water. I was using dead reckoning. Except that I didn't have a taffrail log, so I didn't know how far I had gone each day. Also I made my log entries at the end of the day. Can you see some possibility of error here?

Anyway one calm morning I get the chart out and plot up all my estimates of direction and distance. How confident am I of the outcome? How could I know. It could be 50 miles out in any direction. Also I had not included the effect of the current. However these were my estimates I had some ownership and I plotted a course to intersect the canaries on an oblique angle to maximise my chance of making a landfall. I planned to sail on

240-260 until I reached 14⁰ West, then due South. This meant that I could be 50 miles either side of my planned course when I reached the Canaries and still find a landfall and be OK. I had brought some seeming certainty to my situation.

Three more ships. If this is the container route to Australia then my dead reckoning was a long way off. I want to believe that my dead reckoning was OK. I continue on my course across the shipping lane. I see the vapour trail of a jet going my way. See, I am right and the ships are wrong. As the jet gets close it alters course to go on 195 the same direction as the ships. Let's think this through again.

After much pondering, plotting and examining of charts have decided to abandon my dead reckoning plot. I think it was more than 100 miles out. We shall see eventually how this all turns out. Am convinced that this shipping lane is the one from Bishop Rock to Cape Town and South America. It runs on a bearing of 195 in this region. So am now following the ships and planes on magnetic 205. According to my DR plot I am 380 miles from Gran Canaria. Think it is probably less than that. I will now be in this shipping lane for a week or two. Hope I don't get run down.

Well – have made it through another night. About an hour before dawn was opening a new tin of oats when I saw two white navigation lights right above one another - on an approaching ship. This meant that he was heading directly for me. Dropped centreplate and watched to see if he was pointing to either side. He wasn't. Unleashed tiller and headed off to starboard. Got sails all aback. Not too manoeuvrable with square sails and I have had no practice anyway. Altered the angle of the square sails (this involved adjustment to 12 lines) and headed off to starboard again. The two whites began to separate. 'Twas a big container ship – went past less than 100 yards away. He knew I was there. He had a look with his searchlight as he went past.

Am happy to be heading for the Canaries instead of messing about with navigational finesses. Turned a little left and soon found the shipping lane. Having found the shipping lane which went to the Canaries I was hanging on the edge of it. Each night I would sail out of the shipping lane in order to not be run down. Each morning I would head back towards the shipping lane and follow them South. Don't recall this strategy being mentioned in the navigation books! However it works just fine.

Jan-Olof wrote in 2004 'I have also many times told the story about "the Australian who sailed in the small boat". It differs slightly from what you writes. I think my version is somewhat better. I don´t remember that you had a sextant. Did you really told me that? I was very worried about how you should find Barbados. As I remember it you sailed in zig-zag from Gibraltar to the Canaries for not to miss it.'

According to my noon shot my latitude is 29^0 32'. Ile Graciosa the Northernmost of the Canaries is at 29^0 30'. Seems unlikely. I will get the sextant out and try for a shot of Polaris tonight. Didn't find out till later that twilight was the normal time to shoot the stars. You need to be able to see both the stars and the horizon. However I can tell you that it is possible to get a shot of Polaris in the dead of night.

Jet flew over coming from the Canaries. Am headed in roughly the right direction. Polynesians navigate by observing natural phenomena like clouds, waves and birds. I was doing something similar watching the big birds.

Day 18 The funniest thing has just happened to me. In the dim light of early morning twilight, I thought that I saw a light house. On closer examination I still think that it is a light house. The characteristics appear to be 4 in 12. I expect that it is the one on Gran Canaria about two miles from Las Palmas. Bearing 210. If this is right, my Latitude shot of yesterday was OK and the current has been incredibly strong. Am heading on 210 to see what this is all about.

About that dead reckoning plot, seems I had gone about twice as far as I had thought. My plot had me off Meddouza or not even half way to the Canaries. Yet I arrived two days later. A half knot current for 18 days (18 X 24)/2 – 216 miles plus some drifting during the night. That is probably the explanation. Although my dead reckoning of distance was simply how far I thought I had travelled each day, so it could be (was) way off.

If I had not found the shipping lane and followed it to the Canaries, I would have missed the Canaries altogether and ended up in mid Atlantic. This is the reason that early navigators used to sail within sight of land. Romans would head in the general direction of home and look for the distinctive shape of Mount Vesuvius poking up above the clouds. However it is pretty hard to get lost in the Mediterranean. No point in dwelling on what might have gone wrong. I now had the Canaries in sight, but which island was it?

On the chart the characteristic of the Gran Canaria light is 3 + 1 in 20 – that's near enough for me. Also there are no other lights with similar characteristics in the vicinity. Think I can see the 'tit' shaped top of Gran Canaria thrusting up above the clouds. There has been some whooping and hollering going on around here in the last few minutes.

Evening: am headed for the NE corner of either Gran Canaria or Tenerife, won't know which till I get around the corner.

Saw another island to the South West. I took bearings on both of these islands and consulted the chart. Seemed to me that I was heading between Gran Canaria and Tenerife. Altered course for Gran Canaria. Could see it in the clouds to the SE. Took down square sails and raised the normal browns. The wind was very light and I was feeling the accumulated weariness of the last two weeks. Decided to do the safe thing and anchor off Tenerife for the night. Changed course again and am now slowly edging towards the NE corner of Tenerife. Hope for a good night's sleep tonight and Las Palmas tomorrow.

After dark, the difficulties of finding an anchorage in a strange cove seemed larger and the wind freshened a little, so took down the greens and put up the brown sails. Sailed through the night towards Gran Canaria. It was hell. This blasted body of mine won't even stay operative for 24 hours. Punched it, slapped face, fell asleep and bashed head on the mast, nearly fell out of the boat several times. Still I could not stay awake. Did not want to sea anchor as early on there were many ships. Also would have drifted down wind and current and had to climb back.

The solitary man is invalid because of this wretched obligatory sleep. One would think that when life was in danger that sleep could be postponed for a couple of days. Not my body. It has rights and it asserts them!

Sailed in very light airs through the next day. Still ghosting along after dark when I heard this sound like a large wave breaking close astern. I peered into the darkness and made out this tall black dorsal fin.

This was a killer whale doing some heavy breathing. He would be longer than my boat and many times heavier. I turned out the lantern hoping he would just go away. Where is he now? Suddenly he appears on the other side of the boat. These guys are smart – in the same thinking league as us. What does he want? He could break my boat with a flick of his tail. I remember a story about a cook on board a fishing boat off the west coast of Canada. The cook throws a pot at the killer whale. The whale leaps onto the fishing boat.

Killer Whale – note the large diagnostic large black dorsal fin

I crouch low in the darkness. He surfaces close to the boat again on the original side. Fortunately, the Gran Canaria fishing fleet headed our way. I didn't see him again.

Got into Las Palmas after midnight. Puerto de la Luz is an enormous harbour full of big ships. Oil is duty free and ships are in and out the whole time. All I wanted was a place to drop anchor so I could go to sleep. That proved difficult to find. Eventually tied up to a large ship's mooring buoy and slept.

Gran Canaria

As I emerged from my locker next morning I saw Ed from Driac II rowing across to me. Breakfasted with Ed and Jenny and caught up on the news of who was sailing where, and the harbour and yacht club conventions in Las Palmas. Great to be in the company of friends.

Stanislav on Narcyz – from Poland with $10 to fund the voyage

I was heading for shore along the yacht club dock and saw a small dishevelled yachtie with round, English National Health style spectacles. As we passed he paused and said in an enquiring tone 'Calais'. This was Stanislav Cisek from Poland who I had met in Calais the previous October. He invited me to join him for lunch on his small yacht. Narcyz was about the same length as Donna Elvira, but he had a keel and a cabin. A small *sitting headroom* cabin. We paddled out in his 'Gummy'. This is German for rubber and so is slang for both inflatable dingy and condom. Some room for confusion here.

Stanislav's yacht had a low freeboard (distance from the water to the top of the boat). This is really a yacht designed for sailing on a lake or in fine weather. The steering vane was home made and fractured during a blow in mid Atlantic. Stanislav was in a state of despair for several days. He had been using the self steering to control the boat for months. However you can still get there without self steering, you just have to hold the tiller all day. And so he did. Me too.

Stanislav wanted to celebrate the fact that we were the guys in the tiny yachts who were going to take on the Atlantic. As we discussed the voyage so far he fried up half a chicken and rummaged around the bilges looking for some cognac. He found some very fine cognac. Stanislav had left Poland with $10 US. He had survived this long by accepting gifts from Polish and Russian ships in each harbour and then bartering the length of chain and the bucket of butter for everything else he needed. This lingers in my memory as the best lunch ever. It is because Stanislav produced the finest celebration he could manage. How often, dear reader, has anyone stretched to the edge of their resources to celebrate with you?

I visited him in Poland after I got back to UK. He was very pleased to have visited Machu Pichu. No mean feat for someone travelling without a passport. While in Venezuela, he wrote to his lady friend in Poland to declare his intention of sailing on around the world. She encouraged him to return to Poland. The convention at this time was that a Polish yachtie anywhere in the world can have his yacht taken as deck cargo on a Polish ship back to Poland. Stanislav exercised this option and went home.

The Communist Party wanted to put him in jail for leaving the country without appropriate approval. Fortunately some of his old school mates were high up in the party, knew that he was no threat to anybody and kept him out of jail.

He found that his lady friend was also taking an interest in a mutual friend of theirs. This led to a break-up and a great sadness that he had not continued with his voyage. Unfortunately, beauty kicks in ahead of logic. We are all subject to amorous fantasies, especially when at sea. I was still spending lots of time dreaming about Kerstin.

Peter Frey wrote an article about me in a German yachty magazine with the title 'another lunatic I have met'. Most yachties I met advised me that I was going to die. This view expressed their fear of the Atlantic rather than any serious appreciation of my chances.

Some people lingered longer than required in Gran Canaria. The word would go around that this one was too frightened to take on the Atlantic. Confronted with this reputation, some would sail, others would sell the boat and retreat. There were boats for sale at attractive prices in Gran Canaria.

Another Pole I met was on a large green foam sandwich trimaran. He believed that he could solve the problems of the world. I am not joking, he was writing the book. His flag of nationality was a set of streamers, blue, white, red, green, yellow and black. He averred that these were the colours used in the majority of national flags – he saw himself as the quintessential international sophisticate. The name of the boat ESPOR – educational, social, psychological, you can guess the 'O' maybe organisational research. If you know this guy or his publications send me the contact information, I would like to read the book. The world could do with a little saving.

There were some problems with the crew. (This was true on most boats) Sailing off the coast of Spain the crew of ESPOR became hungry. They were getting a large plate of rice with a few pieces of meat as the main meal of the day. So while the skipper slept they headed in for the coast of Spain. He viewed this as mutiny and got quite excited. They were simply hungry.

Difficult to solve the problems of the world when you can't manage a few people on a yacht. He had been through the war and was accustomed to privation. These were the post war spoiled brats who were accustomed to being comfortable passengers.

In every harbour many crew would find a new skipper and change boats. The crews complained about megalomaniac fascist skippers, the skippers complained about lazy, ignorant, slothful crew. The crew would move to another boat and both parties would then have a similar experience on the next leg of the voyage.

Picture the person who has accumulated the resources to have an ocean going yacht and the time to sail – mature, successful, organised, purposeful. Now picture the young men with time to spare to go sailing - no career, few achievements, laissez faire attitude. It is easy to see that these two groups would have trouble getting along.

Jan-Olof Ronn on Costa Mera was in the harbour. I know that the name sounds like some part of the coast of Spain - close to the Costa Brava perhaps. In fact it means 'costs more' in Swedish.

Jan-Olof on Costa Mera – an accomplished Swedish sailor and great bloke

We played chess and swapped lots of stories. He won the early games, but drank more whisky than me. I was usually winning by midnight. I will get to his 'knife fight in the middle of the night' later.

Cor on Hollander had built his own boat. Took him three years in a shed he rented from a farmer on the edge of town. We were telling jokes one evening, Peter, Cor, Jan-Olof and me (German, Dutchie, Swede and Aussie). All of us had heard all of the jokes in our own language. This was way before the Internet or faxes – the Telex worked just fine.

Pepe and Agneta were the star couple in the harbour. A combination of Swedish cool and Spanish fire. You may be aware that Mediterranean men become excited in the presence of the Northern blondes. A Finnish lady friend described being pursued down the street in Portugal by a young man pleading 'Uno Chocolo, Uno Chocolo' 'one kiss, one kiss'. This contrasted sharply with the cool and diffident approach of Finnish males and she 'melted'.

Was talking to a Czech about the flowering of freedom in Czechoslovakia under the Dubcek regime. Talking of the joy and discovery in the films coming out of Czechoslovakia then. For example 'Closely Watched Trains' which I saw at the Melbourne Film Festival. He said with the European matter of fact acceptance of massive political manipulation of private life. 'Ah that was spring, now it is winter.'

I learned that this part of Spain has a relaxed approach to most things. Drugs were illegal, but freely available from a large ferry-like craft in the middle of the harbour. People were making brief visits to this ferry all day and all night.

Palma was a lovely little town. I spent many convivial moments with the other yachties. Didn't spend much time in the yacht club because I didn't bring my reefer jacket. The yacht club seemed to be the centre of high society. However they allowed us to use their showers and we were grateful for that.

I was invited by the headmaster of the local English language school to dine at his house, halfway up the volcano. We were travelling in his side valve Morris Minor at 30 miles per hour. I was terrified. I had been travelling at 2, 3 and 4 knots for months and this seemed very dangerous. We had a delightful dinner, however after the main course the vine outside the kitchen window started to rattle. He said 'that is the South wind, the harbour is exposed to the South, we must get back to the harbour so that you can move your boat to a safe spot'. We hammered down the mountain. I was the first boat to move. You know what yachties are like. They noticed us move, detected the change of wind and soon all the yachts at anchor were moving in behind the wall of a new, half completed breakwater.

Next day the Spanish police came and tried to force us all to move out into the exposed anchor spot. Strange how the Spanish give control of ports to people who know very little about boats or the sea. One of these Spanish policemen wanted to move us on when we were in the middle of taking the mast out of Stanislav's boat. Difficult to move on when you are standing on the dock holding the mast which is half in and half out of the boat. We stayed in the marina for a few days until the sea and the police calmed down.

Went to the customs house to see if my extra rudder tiller assembly, parell beads etc had arrived. They had. Now I could install the second set of rudder pintles, replace the wired up parell beads and get my boat ready for the Atlantic.

I thought that it would be a good idea to re-paint the bottom of the boat before the crossing. The tide went up and down lots - maybe 15 feet. So I strand myself at high tide and get out the paint brush. The keelboat yachties used to go to a bay on Lanzarote to perform their below the water paint jobs. Mine was much simpler.

Donna in Harbour – Gran Canaria. Note two anchor lines – always two of everything.

Later it was all done and dry and ready to refloat. Some locals offered to help relaunch the boat. They borrowed some wooden chocks with grooves for the keel used by local fishermen to relaunch their boats. Now this was the boat which was to keep me afloat during a 3000 mile Atlantic crossing. I was very careful not to damage or stress it in any way. The locals shouted something in Spanish, half lifted the boat and headed for the water. The chocks upon which the boat was supposed to slide were rotating beneath the boat and banging on the hull. We made the water, but I am left wondering if the hull is damaged.

I was told that after the second world war some Spanish loaded up their open boats with their worldly goods and headed for Venezuela. Picture an open boat with chest of drawers and furniture loaded down to the gunwales, plus the entire family on board. I would be very surprised if any of these boats made it to the other side.

I was ready. Of all the yachties in the harbour, I would be the first to depart, but then I would also take the longest to cross. Some waited months before they plucked up the courage. The decision was simpler for me. I tried to change some Australian dollar traveller's cheques to buy food for the crossing. The Canary island banker said 'what exchange rate do you suggest' meaning 'I won't change your Australian dollars'!

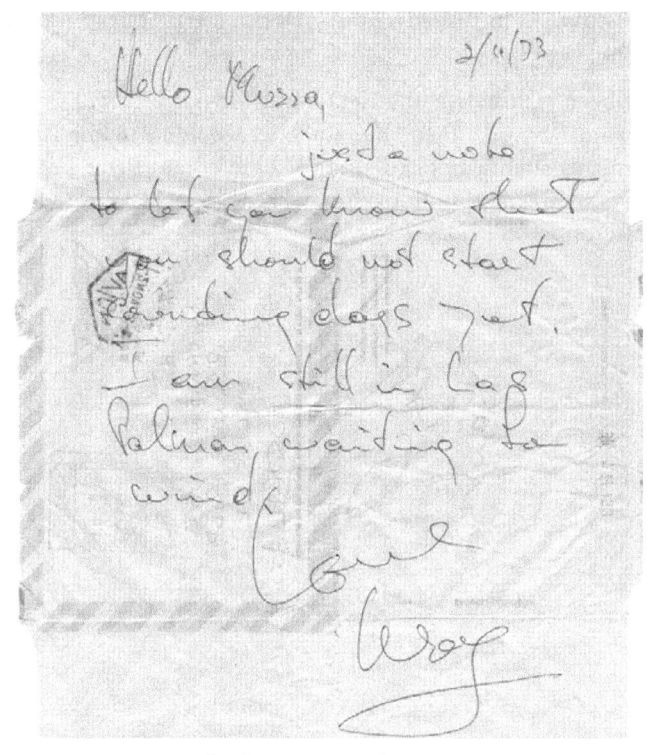

An attempt at a reassuring note

I found an English five pound note in my sporran and went shopping. Lots of Gofio. A Canary Islands special – toasted maize, ground up into a fine brown flour, allegedly very nutritious, certainly very cheap. The local wrestling champion had it in his diet. Also eight tins of meat, high class stuff like Spanish meatballs. Still had some oats and dried milk powder left from the Gibraltar leg. Also some assorted gifts from other yachties, Polish jam, bottle of whisky, and a can of tongue. It might be enough. I didn't know if the crossing would take 30 days or 60 days – it would depend on the wind. If it was 30 days I would have plenty of food.

The hurricane season officially ended on 22 November this was the second. Stanslav pleaded with me to wait a few more weeks. I studied the hurricane chart. Most of the late season hurricanes started on the other side and didn't get anywhere near the Canaries. Doesn't mean it won't happen this year. But then there are lots of risks in this adventure. Besides I was out of money. It was time to go.

I had been waiting for the right wind for nearly a week. Finally the wind arrived, then the anchor wouldn't come up. A fisherman's anchor hooked around some coral. Peter Frey dived down 5 metres and unhooked it. Thank you Peter. At three in the afternoon on Friday 2 November I set sail.

The Crossing

Horns blared and friends waved as I headed out into the Atlantic. I was sad to be leaving all the yachties in the harbour, but it was time to go. You can see in the following photographs that there was a bit of breeze - check the wake. The cardboard boxes in the stern of the boat show that I have just finished loading stores. Steering with the knees suggests that I am getting used to the boat. The baggy wrinkle on the shrouds shows that this is a true cruising yacht.

First a farewell to Peter Frey on Maria Hamburg

Then a wave to Jan-Olof on Costa Mera
Around the breakwater on the right and out into the Atlantic

I had spent quite a lot of time with Peter Frey and Jan-Olof in the Canaries. So I bade them farewell and headed off around the breakwater on the right and out into the Atlantic.

There was no feeling of dread or fear. This is what I had come to do and I was on my way.

I headed away from the coast so as not to get in the wind shadow South of the island. I was taking it carefully and getting the feel of sailing again. Heading South in light wind as it got dark. The motion of the boat had me feeling a little queasy. That would go away in a day or two. I had told my family that I might take 60 days to cross and instructed them not to send a search party. This was my adventure and I would make it or not.

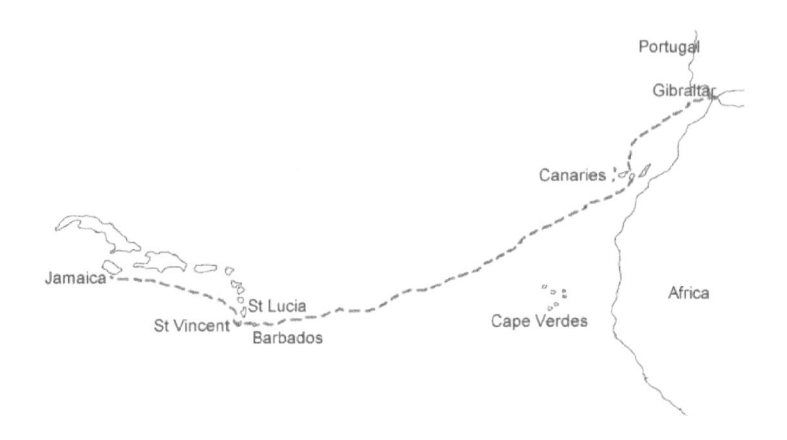

Saw a ship heading my way. I tacked to get out of his path. It was getting closer. I tacked again. The coast was ten miles away. The current went South, even if I could swim ten miles the current would take me past the southernmost point of Gran Canaria and out into the Atlantic. These twin white lights were still getting closer. I tacked again. Couldn't work out what I was doing wrong. Let me tell you this was a crisis – I thought that I was about to be run down and sunk. I tacked again.

A fishing boat went past quite close. This boat had a masthead white and some accommodation lights down low at the rear. The normal for ocean going ships is two masthead whites the forward one lower down. You can rapidly see which way they are going.

As long as the two whites are not above one another, you will be OK. This fishing boat had low accommodation lights on the stern and a masthead white. I thought that he was going this way and he was actually going that. Looking back, seems to me that they may have been coming up to examine my strange little craft. For them it may have been curiosity, for me it was terror.

I sailed on into the night. My plan was to sail South for a couple of days, South West for a couple of weeks and then start taking noon sextant shots of the sun. Contrast this with the contemporary yacht fraternity who spend huge amounts of time gazing at the tiny screen of their Global Positioning System to ascertain exactly where they are and what is the speed over the ground, estimated time of arrival etc. Seems to me that this toy play perverts the yachting experience.

The next few days were spent anxiously scanning the horizon looking for approaching ships and snatching fragments of sleep. I had plenty of time to consider what it would be like to be run down. You wake up to the crash as the boat is fractured against the bows of the ship. The bow wave throws you sideways and you scrape along the side of the ship. If you are lucky you don't get sucked down into the propellers. You are left in a sinking boat as the ship plows on, not even having noticed you were there.

My navigation light was a hurricane lantern sitting on the roof of the locker. Not very high, not very bright but a gesture to help approaching ships notice me. I even trimmed my wick like a wise virgin. I have since discovered that a single white light means 'I am at anchor'. Next time I will get some proper navigation lights. This time, seemed to me being the smallest thing on the ocean that it was my job to get out of the way.

Much more important was my 14 inch radar reflector. Some people seemed to think that a smaller boat should have a smaller radar reflector. Not me. I reckon the smallest boats need the largest radar reflector! Every night I would take down the jib and mount the radar reflector as high as possible on the jib halyard. I hoped that this would keep the big beasties away.

On Majorca I discussed this identification issue with a very pleasant young officer from a US aircraft carrier. He thought that

77

my radar reflector would make a reasonable blip on the screen, but assured me that if they ran me down they would neither know, nor care.

Much of the time I was dreaming about Kerstin.

Longing

Oh my love
I am alone
Yet I have you with me.

My thoughts turn North
In night and day
But cannot bring you to me.

I ask for nothing
Save that you
Spend a short time with me.

I believe
That we will find
Short time should be longer.

That love will grow
With passing day
Ever, ever, stronger

Together we
Can joy create
And satisfaction smoulder.

And maybe even
Procreate
When we're a little bolder.

Too much for now
These forward thoughts
Return to what is true.

I am here
You are there
I long to be with you.

Day 4 Early morning. Have just sent my first morse signal to a ship - .. dah dit dit 'D' I am manoeuvring with difficulty keep clear. He stopped circling me to investigate and went on his way.

While I am grateful for their interest, I try to let them know as soon as possible that I am OK, so that they can get on with their voyage. This was my adventure. I was taking the risk and the responsibility. It did not seem appropriate to divert commercial shipping to deal with whatever problems I might be having. Later when I was out of food I considered asking for help from a passing ship, but still didn't fire the flare.

Have just dined on cucumber, bread, jam and tongue. The tongue reminded me of what used to be called French kissing – now standard fare. Such delights would have to wait. Oats with dried milk powder and gofio, these were the staples of my diet. A Scottish professor of Agriculture from LaTrobe University had assured me that oats was close to a complete food. I was about to test this theory. Well - not a real test - I knew that there might be the odd vitamin or mineral missing from oats, so I took a multivitamin pill every day. Also had some dried milk powder for the calcium. You can see why the touch of tongue was special.

Tuesday was meat day. I know that I am carnivorous. I spent all week thinking about when I could open the next tin of meat. Usually invented an excuse to open it on Monday. Used strong logic such as 'spreading the protein over two days would be better for my system'. I was accustomed to eating well. However when you are going to be a couple of months at sea with no refrigeration and no corner store, the options narrow. I enjoyed bully beef and biscuits on the run between Gibraltar and the Canaries, but that was all gone. I had two kerosene stoves – as always two of everything – but not much that was worth cooking. No problems, I will have a decent feed when I get to the other side.

Making ½ knot on 210. Some fish about. Dressed as usual in shirt 2 jumpers, leather waist coat and Army greatcoat. It is not that cold, but cool enough to justify the gear. When it got a bit warmer I was usually dressed in a T shirt, a Spanish leather hat and nothing else. When you don't wash for a couple of months, ventilation is important.

Nick Grainger who left a day ahead of me from Tenerife reports that he had good wind for the first few days. Didn't happen to me.

I developed salt water sores on the points of my backside (posterior ischial tuberosity – I didn't completely waste my two years of medical school). Not surprising when I was spending ten hours or more per day sitting on the fibreglass deck holding the tiller and steering little Donna. I rummaged around and found the inner tube from a motor scooter which I had brought to soften the seat. It helped a lot, but was more wobbly than you would like.

I tried controlling the tiller with my knee from a standing position. Difficult to stand in my jumpy little yacht. At times it seemed like I was trapped in a mad washing machine. I do understand that having a larger heavier yacht slows the motions down and contributes to the well being of the crew. Other improvements might include, having a shower, a toilet, proper bed, complaisant companion, decent food - some improvements in my situation were possible. Next time .....

Have just discovered a nest of earwigs in my tiny locker. Killed one and three got away. Will do better next time. Rather difficult doing battle inside my three feet wide two feet high locker. Don't want these little brutes dropping on my head. Don't want them crawling on me during the night either. Battled these little beasts for weeks. I am lying in the locker and they are running around 12 inches from my head. Each time I clambered into my sleeping locker, I would take a knife and squish as many as I could. They tried to hide in the cracks of the woodwork, however I eventually got them all.

Some cruising yachties avoid taking cardboard packaging on to their yachts as it could contain cockroach eggs. Some go further and remove the labels from all the tins of food. One yachtie told me how they ended up having mystery dinners, because the hand written description of the contents washed off the tins as they rolled around in the bilges. Some yachties stay away from jetties and docks so that the rats and cockroaches have no chance of getting on board. I had been tied up to lots of docks and had both cardboard boxes and labelled tins. I suppose one nest of earwigs, was getting off lightly. Cockroaches would be a nightmare.

My cool returns

Day 5 Think my cool is returning. I am right in the middle of a shipping lane. Have had ships passing both sides of me all night, yet have had the tiller lashed for hours and had some sleep. A few nights ago as soon as a light appeared on the horizon I began tacking about trying to dodge it. All tonight's ships have been properly lit international vessels, so I can see where they are heading. Also am wearing my radar reflector higher than ever which should mean that they can see me better. This is not the cool of spiked hair, exposed midriff and tight jeans (mindless following of Hollywood originated fashion), but the cool of – seem to be getting to understand this environment and think I will be OK.

Some people seem to think that being in a small boat on a large ocean would produce a state of perpetual terror. Not so. Leaving the harbour is the moment of choice. Once you are on the ocean the immediate environment becomes the entire world. Big questions like 'why am I doing this', 'how will my life evolve' or 'how to make a better world' evaporate in favour of 'do I need to tack to avoid that ship', 'will I put the square sails up' or 'when can I open the next tin of meat'. Most people spend most of their lives dealing with the immediate rather than pondering the profound. It is the same at sea.

Even on the barquentine I sailed on from Jamaica to UK with a crew of 20 the focus was on the immediate. For example what do we do with the two Newfies who get up in the middle of the night, bake bread and hide it in their cabin and attract the rats or shall I drop the main so the squares don't go aback in this 50 knot squall. In the barquentine, if the squares went aback in a 50 knot squall you would probably take out the mast. Clear foreground issues that demand immediate resolution.   No Hamlettian dithering here.

When one is becalmed it is all different. The usual imperatives involved in keeping the boat in working order evaporate and there is nothing to do. This leaves time to ponder the imponderables. I had several bouts of this. I found that I was not a drop out, a hippy or a refugee. I was a problem solver who sought to comprehend the human condition. This approach to life had seen expression as a management consultant and as an actor. It was now being applied to the problem of getting a little boat across an ocean.

Our genes have been pruned to enable us to live in a family, a village or a tribe. Think about what happened to those who didn't fit in. We have not begun to understand how to live in a megalopolis. While it is profitable for manufacturers to have millions of undifferentiated materialist consumers, it is not good for the psyche of the individuals. In Melbourne 30% of people live in one person households. This will not last. We are a group species and will find ways to get together. In any case these solitaries will evaporate from the gene pool.

In a village you know who you are and how you relate to those around you. You know personally the people in power and they can be brought to account. Ants are better than us at living in large colonies, but they have been doing it much longer and within each colony everyone is family.

Think of the people you know who are happy. I suggest that most of them have found a village (golf club, tennis club, political party) to live in. Think of the tormented souls. Do they have a village? I don't think so.

Spent the last half hour being examined by two large dolphins. Many times they surfaced right under my bows. Perhaps they were trying to lead me away. Would love to talk to these creatures. Having no one else to relate to, I ended up thinking of the sea as an unreasonable mistress. Many of my relationships had been with difficult women. This was no accident. Seemed to me that they were less likely to be carrying social diseases than the 'popular' variety.

Why women in the West advertise their physical attributes to every passer by in the street escapes me. How does this exhibitionism help one to find a meaningful relationship? Are they looking for a meaningful relationship? What am I supposed to do with this anatomical detail on the hundreds of women I pass in the street every day? An ex head girl from St Catherine's Girls School explained to me that relationships all start with the lusting carnality, the challenge is to turn it into something deep and meaningful.

Is the world a better place now that we know the exact shape of Madelaine Allbright's fat thighs? Condoleeza Rice in her first outing as Secretary of State had a slit up the back of her right thigh which suggested that she was wearing no knickers. This is a very old fashioned form of diplomacy. Reminds me of Marilyn's 'Happy birthday Mr President'.

Oops, the Larry Summers incident has shown that it is not possible to broach any subject like this without hysteria and vituperous even aspish personal attacks. Anyway it does not have any bearing on the yachty story. Let me retreat with 'it is my view that when the history of this era of great influence on public affairs by women in the West is written we will discover that a great deal more could and should have been accomplished'. Is the 'glass ceiling' an excuse for failure which inhibits further progress.

Realised during the night when my gums felt soft that I had not been taking my vitamin pills. Took two immediately. Very light wind again. If things don't improve I will be lucky if I make Barbados this year. This turns out to be a far sighted observation. It is now November 7. I get to Barbados on 30 December.

I had written to my family saying that it might take 60 days. My hope was that it would be closer to 30. They met on Christmas day and decided that I had gone to the bottom. Such lack of faith. I telephoned them on the 59th day. All the usual stuff about second son and black sheep applies. In their defence, they had a call from America that suggested that I was long overdue.

Have all nerve endings bared. This is the first time I have run down wind at four knots with the square sails up and lashed tiller. If I fall overboard, I will watch the boat disappear over the horizon. Swim about for a while, maybe a day and then, die of thirst or shark attack.

Spent lots of time scanning the environment to see what might go wrong so that I would be ready. I have trailed a line over the stern in the hope that I might be able to grab it if I fall overboard. Some people connect this line to the tiller so that the boat will turn into the wind and stop. I couldn't do this as Donna had no keel and I worried about capsize. The best advice was to 'stay in the boat'.

Sitting on the centreplate housing in the middle of the boat, head and shoulders projecting out of the locker. Should be cat napping draped along the stern locker as usual, but one wave has already climbed in there and doused me. It's getting a bit more vigorous out here.

Should be clear of the shipping lanes in a couple of days. Think I will stay awake tonight as I am not very manoeuvrable with square sails and need to see approaching ships and determine if they are on collision course as early as possible. Sea is steep, short and confused, but not big. Look forward to a few days or weeks time, when the waves will be gradual, long, big and fast. Have just broken out the only bar of chocolate on board. Tonight is crucial, any indulgence is permitted to … 'help me make it through the night'. Was it Carol King who had a hit with this title? 'Come and lay down by my side …'

Lots of moon and whitehorses. Keep thinking I can see ships, but it is only the moon on white water. This is exciting in the most fundamental and wonderful sense. Now I know what it feels like to be in a Trade Wind. My lovely little boat is taking me to Barbados post haste. You may have expected me to know my boat after living in it for a year. Not so. This is new, new, new. I watch all these waves passing beneath my little boat in absolute delight.

Towards midnight, waves now two metres. Still steep and short. Donna lifts beautifully. Three metre cross swell from NW every so often. Donna tilts beautifully. I believe that there is something to be said in favour of 'tender' craft.

Day 6 Have sat up here all night ready to fend off those malevolent monsters called ships. Only now do I see one and he is miles away and not going to get much closer. Am feeling sick after too much chocolate. Have eaten some cucumber to clear the system. Also devoured my second last orange. Still delighted by this wind.

Have just finished my first hot meal for the trip. Now I have some wind I don't have to be so frugal with food. Heated up a can of meatballs. Recommended by Cornelius from Hollander. They were good. As always ate too many. Will be having what's left for dinner, followed by Polish corn coffee with milk and sugar, spiked with whisky. Am now enjoying a pipe of Scotch Mixture. A tiny touch of civilisation.

Wind force two NE. Am making 1-2 knots SW. Expect to spend large parts of today asleep. Am lying in my sleeping bag inside the locker. It is raining outside. My telltale compass says that Donna is maintaining a course approximately SW. Here I lie in mid afternoon, trying to sleep. My body must be short of sleep, but it won't drop off. Maybe it was so overjoyed at getting warm meat for breakfast instead of dry oats or bread and jam, that it is staying awake hoping for more.

Have considered setting a third square sail and decided against it for the moment. Two works well and I will be sleeping much of tonight. Also the third would have to be taken in, in strong winds ie. I must always be watching wind strength because my little boat can be blown over. Two is slower, but will they get me there before my rations run out!

I am running downwind, with the centreplate up and tiller lashed. I am carrying a second rudder tiller assembly. This is following through on the idea that one should have two of everything. Also thought that if I put both rudders in, one behind the other it might provide some directional stability. It did. Donna was being pushed from side to side (yaw) through an arc of 50 degrees. Having just inserted the second rudder I find that the swing is down to 20 degrees. It is like a large skeg on a surfboard. Those experiences at Torquay in the 50s with 'Mumbles' and others as the surfing era was dawning are being brought to account.

My experience of running down wind with square sails is limited. Am trying to go as fast as I can without creating problems. If I can let Donna run through the night then that gathers more miles. Until now I have been taking in the sails at night and having a sleep. People ask me, how did you know where you were in the morning. The reply is that I did not know where I was in the evening, so it is no different in the morning.

Am very glad now that I didn't set that 3rd square sail. Would have had to take it in. Have considered reducing back to one, but think that it will be OK. Am often doing five knots. I worry about being thrown off line by one wave and rolled by the next. Difficult for people who are accustomed to driving cars that are firmly attached to the road to understand how easy it is for the sea to throw a boat about. Keeps one paying attention.

I do not use the centreplate because I fear that the hull will crack next to the centreplate housing. Honnor Marine forgive me. I know that this is a very well built boat. Its just seems to me as I scan my life support system looking for potential problems that this one would be catastrophic. Therefore I minimise it by not using the centreplate at all.

Day 7   The boat has just been thrown off line and a cross sea came on board. I was sitting in the locker hatch. Water in locker, cockpit awash (no draining of any sort – just bailing and sponging). Lashed hatch cover in place, sorted out the mess in the cockpit. Bailed and sponged till it was dry. Then took the tiller for some hours to keep Donna's tail into the seas. I had been trying to sleep all day so I would be fresh for a problem such as this and here I was without sleep feeling quite dopey in the middle of another problem. Still didn't want to shorten sail. Love those five knots. When couldn't stay awake any longer, lashed helm and slumbered along deck. Wet and cold, but I slept.

About midnight conditions moderated a little and I went below and slept in half hour bursts until now. One of the reasons I have such trouble sleeping below is that there are so many strange new noises. Both rudders clank, the water sounds as if it is beating its way through the hull and any loose object anywhere in the boat moves around. However I have now slept a night below while Donna kept reeling in the miles. This is much better than drifting, or lying to the sea anchor.

I have mounted the top two square sails squint, one ten degrees to port and the other ten degrees to starboard, so that when Donna comes off line, one spills wind and the other pushes to bring her back on course. It works! I was about to write some modestly self satisfied comments about my coping when a wave came over the side and drenched me. Maybe this is why I wore a safety line for the first time.

Today the ocean seems vast and Barbados a long way off. The sideways jerk of the boat makes me careful to ensure that I do not fall overboard. Tried some Gofio with water and jam for morning tea. It is good. Wondered what I was going to do with three jars of Polish jam, now I know. Tried to rig the jib as a spinnaker. Not successful. This is not the place for first time attempts with elaborately rigged sails.

Day 8 Sighted a ship. Who said that they stayed in shipping lanes! Ran last night without a light!

The salt water sores and rash have returned to my sitting area. This combined with the constant jerking, rolling and wobbling make it painful to sit. So spent much of yesterday and all of last night supine (flat on my back). It now hurts to lie down as my bed is the floor boards. Who said that it was good for your back to sleep on boards? I have been doing it for six months and it still hurts. A little pain ... a little pleasure.

One week sailing. All I can see is a circle of blue. Having a pleasant day. Have just completed rigging my third square sail. Lash the sail to a spar, connect the sheets to each corner, thread the sheets through blocks and back to the cleats and attach the halyard. I use the same technology the square riggers did 100 years ago. Still works.

Am reading Shakespeare – Merry wives of Windsor. An early comedy. More slapsticky than I expected. A Welsh priest and a French doctor have their accents mocked unmercifully. Is this politically correct? Padriac McGuiness in 'The Australian' observed that the believers in political correctness are predominantly lower middle class, semi educated teachers and journalists who need a simplistic recipe to apply to life because the reality is much too complex.

Day 9 Gums are bleeding already. Think that it is 'cause of lack of apples etc to caress the gums. Have changed brands of vitamin pills to see if that helps. A hidden benefit of this day of fasting is that I am now longing for some Gofio! Gofio is OK but to be longing for it is unexpected. Fast only lasted 16 hours. I was hungry and besides it was getting dark (almost a quote from Thurber).

The almost full moon is shining. There is a gentle breeze and a gentle swell, some cumulous cloud and all is well with the world. Have just had some Gofio with the last of a bottle of jam. For lunch had some Gofio mashed up with sardines. For dinner will have - not gofio - oats. Maybe some meatballs on Tuesday or Wednesday. Today's 'f' word is food.

Am re-reading Blainey's 'Tyranny of Distance'. Still an excellent piece of history, exploring the impact of remoteness on Australia early development. Have dug out the chanter and am attempting some scales. Am not accustomed to reed instruments. This one certainly does not give me good vibrations. I don't have the music gene, but out here who cares.

There were some fish around before. I have two lines out. Poised hung over the gunwale harpoon in hand for some considerable time. The way this toy yacht jumps around it is difficult not to end up in with the fishies.

Just thought of another Shakespearian quote I ran across when at University:

> 'Would that there were no age
> twixt seventeen and three and twenty,
> for there is nothing in the betwixt
> but rioting, shooting, fighting,
> quarrelling with one's elders and
> getting wenches with child.'

It has always delighted me when reading Shakespeare, to discover how relevant he is to the contemporary scene.

Sometimes think of the businessmen who stayed home in Australia and got rich during the war. One of these businessmen boasted to me how he had tooled up to produce the 303 shells in an inefficient way, agreed the price with the government, then retooled in a more efficient way and made piles of money throughout the war. Also think of the British aircraft manufacturers who refused to build aircraft during the early months of the war as they were haggling over price. Churchill threatened to have them shot. Contrast that with my father who crossed the world to throw his life away.

Australia has had privileged elites throughout its history. Problem is they have not deserved their position. What was the criteria for their appointment? Originally they were failures from England given power in the colonies. Australia has been slipping down the economic league table for more than 100 years. This is because these Neroesque elites in Australia have been having a jolly time celebrating their own importance in exclusive clubs rather than helping Australia earn its place in the world.

Allow me one specific example – since World War II there has been a massive expansion in international trade. Most of this was in 'elaborately transformed manufactures'. Where was Australia? Asleep at the stick as usual. Prospering in the short term on exports of wool, wheat, iron ore and coal and taking no regard for the future. In the 1960's Australia made more cars than Japan. In the 1960's Australia exported more cars than Japan. Where is Australia in the car industry now – nowhere. Where is Japan – several global companies. Hence Neroesque – fiddling while the future of the country burns.

Allow me one more example. Two of the first ten computers built in the world were built in Australia. Did you know that Prime Minister Menzies diverted the funding to rain making! We failed in this new industry by deliberate and stupid policy decision. Makes you proud to be Australian.

In 2005 even the mining companies are being sold to foreigners. Australia is like a banana republic that can't even harvest its own bananas.

Who cares? Normal Aussies are more concerned with who is going to win the Saturday's football match or whether the surf is up than any of this esoteric nonsense.

Still have force two NE and am proceeding at two knots SW. Have you ever tried packet chicken soup mixed with cold water and swallowed. It passes the nutrition test if not the taste test. Latitude very roughly 22.

Forever dreaming of Kerstin.

Together

I sleep
with you beside me
I have you
on my mind

I long to
bring you sailing

to see what
we can find

The ocean
it is beautiful
The sky
ere changing charm

The ports are
full and interesting
with friendships
new and warm

But us
my love together
that's what
I desire

Sharing
Understanding
With hearts
and souls on fire

One day
It will happen
We will
be as one

Talking
Laughing
Touching
All our waiting done.

Bombard said to me that navigation was important as knowing one's position was good for morale. He is again right. Have taken a very rough latitude shot - it makes me feel lots better. Am now planning how much latitude I must lose each day after I have turned right. 'South West for a couple of weeks.'

Had a good night. Donna made three to five knots most of the night. Am now doing three knots on 265. Have started to head West as want to be able to use my square sails all the way. When sailing with the jib and main I have to hold the tiller and drive the boat all day. Don't give me this 'need to be needed stuff'. I am delighted to be able to lash the helm and do other things. Lêves time for pondering and scribbling. Have you noticed that the widely observed conventions regarding the use of flattery and cliche recede when alone.

Flying fish 1.5 inches long on board this morning. Am looking forward to having his big brother for breakfast one of these mornings.

Nice drop of rain during the night. Seem to get a shower every night. Wind always acts up just after sunset. Last night, wind went 'puffy' and the sea went 'lumpy'. Something to do with the boundary between light and dark, warm and cold. The interesting stuff is always at the boundaries. Or to quote from Peter Schaffer's Equus, 'the extremity is the point'.

Latitude- again not too accurate some cloud – 20^0 44'. Think I just saw my first shark. Have been expecting to see sharks or whales for some time now. I suppose he is still around, but doesn't seem to want to show himself.

Aegre in mid Atlantic

Nick Grainger took this photo in mid Atlantic by swimming 30 metres away from the boat with camera held high. It must have been during one of the multi day calms. The most frustrating time is when there is no wind and the rigging rattles and slaps. I reckon that he must have had an attack of cabin fever. I asked him about sharks. He said that he hadn't seen any for a couple of days! Well I didn't have a camera and besides there was no way I was going in the water. Taken by a shark would be an absurd way to die.

Sharks

Sharks have tiny brain but a great sniffer. Put some blood in the water and the sharks will be there momentarily (in a moment is the American sense, for a moment in the English sense – both true) to see what is for dinner. I am very impressed with the design of the shark, a very old and very refined species. My dentist friends tell me that the shark supplies its own fluoride to keep all of those teeth healthy. They can turn in their own length and accelerate quickly. They are masters in their own environment. Well, not completely.

Dolphins don't like sharks. Perhaps for the same reason as me. The sharks eat their lunch. A pack of dolphins (at least four) will ambush a shark, surround it so that it cannot get away and then butt it firmly in the abdomen to cause internal bleeding which means that the shark will die some hours later. The dolphins can travel at 40 km per hour. Am told that you can swim with no fear of sharks when there are dolphins around. Not me. I did not go in the water at any point on this crossing. The sharks were ten feet long and terrifying.

Stay in the boat

Fairfax when rowing the Atlantic and the Pacific would lassoo the sharks, attach them to his boat and drown them. Sharks need water passing over their gills or they cannot get the oxygen required to sustain life. I thought about doing this but worried that they may be strong enough to overturn my boat. At that point I would become their lunch.

Day 11 Sorry I could not write until now, had to get some meat balls inside me. Seems like I have not had meat for years! Very little wind. That crazy 1-2 foot chop which I hated in the Med is here. These are the worst possible conditions for a tender little boat like Donna. She jerks about incessantly like a demented washing machine. Tipped the pan of meat balls off the fire and tipped the stove and kettle over. At least I am getting some meat.

Very little wind during the night. Took lines forward from the superior square sail yard to try to stop the flogging. Considered taking all sail in, but we are making a quarter to a half a knot and I like progress. Have some small fish around the boat, will try to catch them later. As Bombard advised, the fish come to the boat when you are becalmed. Great to have a mobile pantry.

Have always felt when reading sailing books that yachties let themselves get too obsessed with where they were and when they would arrive. Why not just 'be' and enjoy the scene. While I do some 'being', I also do an awful lot of pondering about where I am, when will I arrive, what will be in the mail, what I will eat and who will be there.

Latitude 20^0 32' (pretty accurate – I think). Still very little wind.

Have developed a great thirst which I am trying to control. Maybe because I put salt water in with the meat balls when frying them. Strikes me as curious that I have volunteered for this experience which many people would avoid at all costs. However I am very clear about two things – stay afloat and make as much distance in the right direction as possible. Nice to have some truths to cling to.

Have NW wind and am heading South. Could take down the square sails and mount the 3 cornered but won't unless the wind persists for some time.

Well the meat balls are finished. Seem to have the gobbles lately. If it had been possible to lick the pan without sticking my beard in the goo I would have. Also these last two days have been downing two litres of water per day. Until now have restricted myself to one. One litre is not enough, as I was discovering!

Still reaching SSW with three squares as darkness falls. I was warned before embarking on the Atlantic that the Trades blew at a constant force 5, some said force 7. I have been out here for two weeks and have had nothing greater than 4, often 1-2. Reading 'Ocean Passages for the World' years later, realised that the wind and current are stronger further South. This means that one should head down towards the Cape Verde Islands before turning right. I shall return.

I should eat well more often. Am full of bounce and joy. Morale best it has been so far this voyage. 'tis close to midnight. Here I sit. Have taken down square sails. Wearing mizzen only. Beautiful moonlit night. Nice steady swell. Very little wind. Shall sleep shortly. 'tis pleasant just sitting and pondering. Polaris is in fact a hands breadth above the horizon – a traditional indicator of when to turn right.

Still can't sleep so have lit Tilley lantern and hung it over the side of Donna to see what I can attract. So far there are half a dozen baby eels or sea snakes about two inches long which keep flinging themselves at the boat trying to get to the light. Also four eight inch somethings who spend most of their time under the boat and come out for a look every now and then. Hope I don't attract anything too big!

Day 12 Two hours after dawn. Have just woken with that didn't sleep properly weariness. Still no wind! Am breakfasting as usual, on oats. Late morning – now a nice gentle breeze from the SSW. Reaching West at half a knot under jib and mizzen. Better than drifting North. Although there is very little doubt that the Trades will return and I will proceed to Barbados in reasonable time, one becomes acutely aware that one's supply of food and water has a limit. Would love to go for a walk, eat some fruit, talk to somebody.

People told me that the winds in December were more reliable. However I was in Las Palmas, unable to cash my traveller's cheques and not eating very well. The sooner I left, the sooner I would arrive on the other side. Even if the trip was a bit longer. So here I am with SSW wind making very slow progress.

Latitude 20^0 05'. The sun is very hot. Two hours to sunset. Hallelujah for the king of beasts, that extraordinary predator man.

I have three beautiful fisheys in my cockpit. Have been trailing a line much of the way here and sporadically trying to harpoon fish. Tried harpooning today with no success. So got my small hook line and sinker and dandled this beside the boat. Had fifteen fish rushing round and several almost strikes. Tried baiting the hook with a piece of white plastic bag. This disappeared. Fitted another hook and lighter sinker and tried again. More frenzy. Then noticed that they were trying to eat the sinker. Maybe it looked more like a fish.

I had read about a French yachtie probably Alain Gerbault on an Atlantic crossing in the 1920's who dandled his toes in the water to attract the fish before spearing them. So grabbed my King Neptune harpoon, lowered it to about the same depth as the sinker and got them going again. This depth issue is crucial. It is difficult to gauge from above. In fact I was using the sinker to bring the fish to a known depth so that I could spear them with a lunge of the forearm. Was momentarily stunned into inaction when my harpoon sank into the first one. 'Everything comes to those who wait', bon appetit et merci Dieu.

The fish was beautiful. Merely fried in salt water and a little oil, but beautiful. Was throwing the scraps over the side as I ate and other fish were coming up very close to eat them. Unable to resist this, while still cooking, I tossed the scraps so they sank to the right depth just next to me and used my trident again. Now have one cooked and two beheaded and gutted. Just in case I get some wind and can't fish for a while. It is now an hour after dark and I feel quite tired. My boat smells like a dirty fish shop and will be worse tomorrow. Must tidy up some of this mess and pray for wind. Bonne soir.

Darkness time: Thought the sharks would be around. Blood in the water attracts them. There is one under the boat right now eating my little fish – the ones who are pressing themselves against the bottom of the boat to escape his jaws. He keeps bumping the boat and rubbing himself on keel and rudder. About six feet long. Often with dorsal fin sticking well out of the water right next to the boat. I have tidied up and am having my end of day pipe. I shall continue, don't need any shark meat right now.

Just worked out why these small fish hide under my boat. Sharks normally attack from the deep in one swift motion. The fish under my boat are not visible to the shark below and hence less likely to be attacked.

Middle of the night: Have wind with some East in it, so have set two squares and am making one knot West.

Day13   Up one hour before sunrise.   Making one knot 295 Haven't been sleeping very well these last few nights. Felt 'up tight' can't drop off to sleep. Also woke up several times during the night with dry mouth. The good news is that my constant feeling of hunger is gone since I had some fish. Today was to be fast day. Instead it shall be a fish feast day.

'To him that hath shall more be given'. While eating my fishy breakfast this morning, one piece didn't appeal to me so I hooked it on the hook with a two inch white feather lure, six inches of rigid rusty wire and a bright orange - large gauge - hand line and trailed it astern. Have just pulled it in to find a brilliant yellow two foot six inch fishy on the end. He didn't want to die. Kept trying to bite me. Turned a bright white as he died and is now a blotchy yellow and white.

I am not much of a hunter. One three inch fish when I was aged ten. Two Kangaroos and two rabbits on a drunken Christmas shooting spree. Two parrots with an airgun. Suddenly here I am knocking off fish like one thing. I now understand why John Fairfax lassoed sharks:
- they are such frightening creatures
- they eat my tomorrow's lunch
- it relieves the boredom of being out here.
- it is interaction of a kind.

'tis very hot and very little wind. My fish are drying in the sun and I am trying not to. New water container started yesterday. (4 gallons in 14 days, 16 litres) Was going to begin looking for ships in the NY Cape of Good Hope shipping lane tomorrow. But since I have been making such small progress will defer that until Monday.

Just read an article by L. Von Bertalaffy 'The theory of open systems in physics and biology' Science Vol III (1950) pp 23-9 It expands the static models to address the interaction with the environment. It was available before I started my secondary schooling. Yet there was no indication of its impact at school or during two years of my medical course. Teachers prating out of date ideas with great authority? Never.

Dead of night: Have just lit a candle in my little locker for the first time. It is a beautiful soft warm light and makes me feel good. Later, fashioned a lovely candlestick holder with a piece of wood and a tin lid. Can now do a full scale Wee Willie Winkie. If I had enough candles I would be tempted to make a gymballed chandelier. A smidge of elegance in mid Atlantic.

More Oats

Day 14 Breakfast – oats and fish. Morning tea – oats. Lunch – Gofio and jam. Afternoon tea – oats. Dinner – oats and fish. The tin of oats I opened this morning had a large cover of mould where the salt water had got to it. Probably in that 'blow' off Casablanca. Hope the remaining tins are OK. Would be a shame to run out of oats!

Have put out my fishing line with a four inch wooden imitation fish on the end and three, three prong hooks well baited. Real fishermen may find my approach naive. I just wanted to get something to eat.

Two weeks. Not much progress in the first few days, or in the last few, but I must have made some miles in that middle week. All I can see is a circle of blue and a few clouds. Am heading a bit North of West. Would have to take down squares and put up main and jib to get back on 260 or 270. Shan't bother today. Maybe tomorrow if this idiotic wind persists.

Day15 Had a jet overhead during the night. Also noticed some fish almost within harpoon range. Got the trident into one, but he scrambled off. A large school of porpoises went past about a mile away. All leaping out of the water and doing belly whackers. I could use someone to play with.

Rose an hour after dawn to find dark threatening skies and wind increasing from the West! Wind became quite strong. Lashed a few things on deck. Streamed the sea anchor, shortened mizzen and scrambled into the locker as the rain arrived. There is lots of rain, should be out there taking a shower or collecting water. But it is warm in here. Shall have a pipe and think about the situation.

Have just finished an exquisite breakfast. How often does one have fish that is in the frying pan before it has gone cold. Seemed to be only one Dorado around the boat. Now there are none.

Wind has gone around to North and is very light. One day the Trades will blow. Late Morning Very light wind from the SE. Haven't bothered to set any sails. Have decided that the main mast rigging is the next most vulnerable part of my ship. The anchor points for the back stays are merely bolted through the fibreglass seat with small nuts and washers. In Barbados will install backing plates, probably a running backstay and perhaps shrouds. Probably twin forestays also. The definition of the perfect boat continues to evolve. Perfect for what? Perfect for single handing is quite different to perfect for a crew of six.

Met an Englishman who crossed the Atlantic with a reef in the main. He could have used full sized sails all the way. He kept it small, so he wouldn't have to do any work in mid Atlantic. He didn't like yachties, or talking about sailing. When asked why do you sail he said 'it's the only way my wife won't travel'.

Have just been visited by some sharks. Difficult to work out what kind or how many from the assorted views of dorsal and tail fins I had. Tried to tempt them closer with some of this morning's fish, but they were not having any.

Twilight time: Have dined for a change on oats and fish. Am having a quiet smoke with one of my other pipes I found while digging around today. Wind SW 1-2 useless. Squalls and variable winds feels like the doldrums. Shall take another latitude shot tomorrow and confirm that this is not possible. The pilot chart gives the northern limit of the Trades in December as 25^0 N. I think that I am between 20^0 and 21^0 N. Ergo I should have a force 4-5 NE wind six to ten foot following sea. Am looking forward to that.

Day16 Almost midday. Am taking sun sight. Has been - still is - two metre old regular long swell from Magnetic 290 and two foot wind produced fresh short chop from mag 215. Have hung to sea anchor all night and morning. 'If I can't have sensible winds, I won't sail!'

Latitude 21^0 40'. Not too accurate as Donna is leaping about like a dervish. Shall head SW when I can. Sailed for a few hours in the afternoon to the SE. Only made a knot and the black clouds were overtaking me anyway. Had worked out that I was on the southern edge of a low and was trying to sail out of its influence. Have found that my wandering mind meanders better when I have the tiller in my hand.

However dropped sail at approximately 1600 hours, put out sea anchor and continued reading Antony and Cleopatre. Was overcome by queasiness so went to bed. Gut still wouldn't get happy, so administered some medicinal scotch. Am now growing voluble under the influence of said 'Black and White'. Truly the nectar of the gods. (Venus has just disappeared behind a black cloud.) Gut is now in order. In fact whisky has proved most medicinal. A friend in Gibraltar quoted his dad who had worked for Shell all around the world saying that 'anyone who says you shouldn't drink alone – has never been alone'.

Well, this week of calm means that however long it was going to take me to reach America, it will now take a week longer. Another week of oats and Gofio! Maybe I am beginning to understand Sir Francis Chichester's tendency to imbibe whisky before he went out to change the sails. Anything to spice up the routine.

Intend to fast tomorrow to let the gut sort itself out. Can't decide if it was the fish or the fact that I did not manage to eliminate all of the mould from the oats. Maybe the gut is merely demanding some more Black and White. That's easily remedied.

Wind is force 1-2 from 240 and whisky continues to be delightful. Why am I out on this goddamn ocean when I would rather be in Sweden with my lovely Kerstin. Right now I don't have an answer to that question, nor any remedy to the situation – 'cheers'.

How should one deal with a world that is full of blather and hypocrisy. We all recognise that the exercise of power is the ultimate reality. Ivan Illich (who spoke at a meeting I attended in Melbourne in 1972) says that the South Americans could much more readily accept subjugation to North America, rather than this curious preaching that low fertility and many material things will produce the TRUE happiness (emptiness). He points out that peasant South America can endure enormous hardship and extreme poverty with dignity. In the conspicuous consumption ethic, there is little dignity, just a rat heap. Lower yourself to scrapping with the rats and you have become one.

You can see that sitting alone in the middle of the ocean the world's problems can be clearly understood and solved at a stroke. I have cut a great deal of this material from the log because I thought that not everyone would enjoy it. Allow me to let this one run for a little.

How have we evolved to this position where any jerk with money is supposed to have the pick of the chicks and does of the commercially available chicks. Notice the well groomed blondes in the affluent suburbs. Is it true that there are still some who are looking for love? Let's hope so.

Now there have always been women who do it for the money – the oldest profession. There are plenty more whose choice of man is influenced by the size of his ... wallet. These too are members of the profession.

For most of our evolution there have been conventions in the tribe or village which allowed workable pairings to take place. Even the very primitive New Guinea tribes-people who killed members of neighbouring tribes on sight most of the time, would meet for bride swapping once a year. Traces of these conventions lingered in Western culture through to the 1950s. Now we have abandoned them in favour of an atomised society where being a standardised compliant consumer of material things is the norm. This leaves each individual woman to bargain for the best price she can get for her beauty. Check any bar. Is this progress? Is it even civilised? It is not however new. Shakespeare said: 'Beauty is nature's currency and must be spent'.

Jan-Olof Ronn from Sweden took a Canadian engaged couple on board in the Canaries as paying passenger crew for the voyage to Barbados. The bloke knew nothing about sailing but was co-operative and in that blokey way learnt quickly and was of value. The female on the other hand thought that she knew all about everything, to quote Jan-Olof - from an interview we did together on Barbados radio – 'she wanted to gybe the spinnaker in the middle of the Atlantic with a cigarette hanging out of the side of her mouth'.

The tension built between the Canadian woman and the skipper. She was seeking to assert dominance on his boat. She would insist that he said 'excuse me please' before she would move her knees out of the way so that he could walk from one end of the cabin to the other. Late one night his irritation with this procedure caused him to swat her out of the way. The Canadian bloke pinned the Swede's arms for assaulting his woman. The chick grasped a pot of close to boiling water from the stove and flung in Jan-Olof's face. She then grasped the carving knife and came towards him. He struggled free ran to the forward hatch, clambered onto the deck and scrambled back to the cockpit.

'Now I have a knife too, what are you going to do!' The debate lasted for hours. Eventually the Canadian guy was declared umpire and threw both knives into the sea. As if that would solve the problem!

Jan-Olof wished to bring this misadventure to the earliest possible conclusion. Beating back to the Canaries was impractical, so he turned left and headed for the Cape Verde Islands. When he arrived he went to the local authorities seeking assistance. 'I have these crazy people on my boat – we had a sort of knife fight in the middle of the night'. They reminded him that whatever detritus a skipper brings to a port he is responsible for removing. Jan-Olof paid for the couple to spend a week in a hotel and two airfares back to Europe. Some other yachties thought that he should have just lifted the pick, sailed away and left them to it. He was a responsible citizen and had to resolve the issue before sailing. What would you have done?

My stomach has improved to the point where I can and shall indulge in a pipeful of MacBarens Scotch Mixture. Quite often I awake from whatever thought, to realise that I am in a little boat in the middle of the Atlantic and it strikes me as unreal and a little bizarre. One is quietly reading Shakespeare or merely meditating and suddenly awakes to the fact that land is one month away. If this wind persists that land will be Africa not America. Maybe I should turn around and sail to Sweden and Kerstin.

Shark is bashing about under the boat. Clambered out of the locker to inspect this brute. Think he was big - he was bending in the bottom of the boat. Made a strange scraping sound as he grated on Donna's bottom. I have this fear that some large sea dwelling creature will destroy the boat. Not likely but possible. A giant squid or a killer whale would have no trouble despatching little Donna. Fortunately this shark seems happy to just eat the fish hiding under the boat.

Day 17 Been reaching South since dawn. Saw one shark and had one bounce off the rudder. Still feel strange in the gut, haven't eaten. Am starving.

Day 18 Mid morning. Am making half a knot with three square sails. At this rate I will go a long way in an extraordinarily long time. Otherwise everything in the garden is lovely. Dorados and flying fish leaping about. Again a shark visit during the night. Am currently consuming a Bowyers tongue and turkey roll. Best fodder I have had for some time.

How is your Shakespeare? Did you know that Julius Caesar 'ploughed Cleopatra and she cropped'? What about – 'age cannot wither her, nor custom stale her infinite variety'. This is the short and scrawny Cleopatre with large hooked nose and rotten teeth. Girls forget the mirror and go for attitude!

Have since discovered that Cleopatre was 21 when she first visited Rome and stunned the Romans with Egyptian pomp and style. This was about the time when Caesar had his liason. Their earliest meeting in Alexandria was when Cleopatre had herself smuggled into his presence concealed inside a carpet. He was both startled and delighted when Cleopatre emerged as the carpet was unrolled. Maybe it was Antony much later, back in Alexandria who got the rotten teeth. Not that she slept around. Candidates had to be actual or possible emperors of Rome. Not sure about siblings.

At last I am making more than one knot in the desired direction. Wind is freshening – would you believe from the NE! Whoever heard of NE winds in the NE trades belt? Maybe I will get to the West Indies this year.

Have just soldiered through chapter two of Nimzowitsch. Good stuff but difficult going. Should play brilliant chess in Barbados.

The large long old Westerly swell that rolled past me for the last four days could have been, probably was, produced by strong winds blowing for a long time - perhaps a hurricane – they do occur at this time of year.

I hope I notice the shipping lane (New York – Cape Town) when I cross it as that would mean that I was more than half way. My other means of getting a very rough Longitude is to take a bearing on the setting sun. If my compasses are still accurate to the deviation card prepared in Gibraltar I will be able to read off an approximate Longitude on the chart. Most days there was cloud around the horizon at sunset so my position stayed a mystery.

Am going to try to drag my water consumption down to one litre per day. I have:
- 17 tins of oats,

- 4.5 kilos of Gofio
- 1.5 jars of jam
- 1 tin of biscuits
- 3 packets of chicken soup
- some dried milk
- 6 small cubes of cheese
- 3 jars of coffee (for the fishes) and
- as many dorados as my harpoon can spear.

You may say that I could consume two litres of water per day. Some factors:
- 25 may be oily and undrinkable (cleaned the jerry can many times but am not sure that it was enough)
- What happens if one of my canisters gets holed or disappears overboard
- who knows how long I shall be out here.

Day 19   Midday (plus a bit), Latitude 19⁰ 54' N   Wind is slowly increasing from the NE. Am now doing two knots. The fish who like to be under the boat can't keep up when I go too fast – as Bombard told me.

So, just in case tomorrow is a good day for sailing and bad for fishing, I cut some bait from the Dorado kept for that purpose, baited the hook and was untangling the line with only about four feet out when the bait was taken. The line can stay tangled. Now have fresh Dorado for supper. Won't bother to behead or clean this one merely take two large steaks off his back, an extra bit for next time's bait and throw the rest away. Filleting is a frightfully messy business.

Perhaps it was decaying fish that gave me tummy ache a few days ago, so from now on will only eat fresh caught and fresh cooked. The sun - as usual - going down surrounded by cloud so that I cannot get a bearing. Quel domage.

Sinking

As I lay down on the floorboards to sleep, the boat rolled and I was floated up by large amounts of water in the bilges. Sinking in mid ocean! First things first, lets make sure we can get water out faster than it is coming in. Bailed frantically for some time. The water level was going down. Bailed some more and then began to look for the source of this problem.

The boat is divided into four compartments, forward hole, locker, cockpit, stern lockers. Had made some attempt to isolate these from one another. Had not tested it so I did not know the exact state of affairs. Well I knew about the bits I had built. While bailing the locker was thinking that perhaps the centreplate housing had cracked near the hull. This is a constant anxiety for me and would have presented formidable problems.

The inspection revealed:
- Forward hole – almost dry
- cockpit seemed OK
- Stern Lockers – almost full.

Here was the source of the problem. Earlier in the day I had taken my hand bearing compass out of this locker. It was in a plastic box which was propping up a hose. The bilge pump had been moved to a more convenient location leaving the hose - which communicated directly with the outboard well - low enough to let water in. While its entry point was normally above the water line, I had a steep short following sea which was sending water in. I think that is what it is all about. However I shall not sleep for a few more hours, if at all, till I see that all is well. Have bent the hose back against the roof of the locker. Will plug the hole and seal it tomorrow. Have decided that I will not have skin fittings (anything which communicates through the hull) on my next boat.

A doctor friend of mine who is also a yachtsman says that the problem with doctors, motor mechanics and yachtsmen is that they don't make a precise anatomical diagnosis. I have made mine, but will stay around to check. Can't afford to be wrong. Throughout all of this Donna has been and still is making 1-2 knots SW. A lovely little boat.

Day 20   Latitude 19^0 16' Wind holding, sea slowly building up, but still disordered. Making two knots 280.

Late Afternoon: Have just found a flying fish on board. As I don't know how long he had been there, I consigned him to the deep. Have just shifted a five gallon bottle of water from forward hole to cockpit. The nose had seemed to be lower than it should have been. Hope this will be the cure. Also filled lamps and stove with paraffin. Today I feel as if I could sail around the world four times without eating, sleeping or drinking. Am coming to believe that diet has a strong effect on morale. What a revelation! In the last 24 hours have consumed all of my cheese.

Day 21 Latitude 19^0 28' Speed varies between zero and a quarter of a knot. Mid Afternoon: Harpooned a small fish. The question is, is it edible? Don't want to be poisoned. It reminds me of a spine fish or stone fish. Can't afford to take the risk, will use it as bait for a Dorado. On second thoughts threw it overboard. To catch fish and not eat it is a shame. I am very hungry.

The end of week three and I am not even half way. Normal yachts take four weeks to cross. Have streamed line for Dorado again, but don't expect any success today.

Imagine how Bombard must have felt on his diet of fish, plankton and sea water. I crave anything fresh. I dream about beautiful fresh bread and butter. Isn't that crazy. Think of myself running down the street in Barbados buying some bread and butter and eating it on the spot. Then making tomato and onion sandwiches. To feel the crunch and taste the sharpness of the onion, then the crispness of the bread and underneath the flavour of tomato, plus lots of pepper and salt. Yum.

Very slow again today. Its going to be a loooong voyage. Come on its already been a long voyage. My longest anyway. Hauled the forestay tight with block and tackle earlier. Has steadied the mast up a bit. The incessant rattle and slap, rattle and slap, rattle and slap that fills the air when becalmed can be very irritating!

Dusk: Find that the 'sealed' compartments on either side of the cockpit are full of water. This must be how the water got from the stern lockers to the main locker. I am ever more adamant that my next boat will be built with my own hands so that I know exactly the wheres, whys and whats of its construction and can rapidly diagnose and fix any problems.

The Swedes have a saying that you could sail downwind on a haystack. This could be translated as 'keep it simple'. No deep skegs, towering masts, wide hull or open cockpit. What about a length of sewer pipe 3 metres wide and 11 metres long? I could get around the world in such a craft.

Don't laugh, I am about to build a model to test this idea. One virtue of such a design is that it is unlikely to be damaged by a large wave dropping on it. Seems to me that this possibility is ignored in the design of many modern yachts. Remember priority one, two and three are to stay afloat. There is no rescue chopper in the middle of the ocean.

Not sleeping so came on deck. Glanced around the horizon, thought that I saw a ship. But I have thought that many times lately. There are low stars and there is lots of phosphorus in the sea. Donned shirt, jumper and glasses and looked again. It is a ship! I know that won't seem important to you but to me it is enormously important. I may be half way there. Have to see more ships before I believe that this is the shipping lane, rather than a maverick who is going somewhere other than New York. He is heading NW though, that's as it should be.

Joy and fear possessed me simultaneously. Joy because it may be the shipping lane and at least it is a sight of something human. Then the old fear of being run down. These ships really have me terrified. Had to grab the toilet bucket. Then removed the second rudder, inserted mizzen mast and connected sheet. Hanked on jib. All in preparation for evasive action if necessary. Am now perched on deck scanning the horizon to see if there are any more.

Day22 Latitude 19^0 25' Making 2-3 knots 260

Day 23 Good morning folks. Last night the real trade winds arrived and I had to shorten sail. In fact I shortened sail three times during the night. Rose this morning about dawn, was sitting in the hatch waking up, getting ready to put my shirt on, when a wave came over the stern and gave me a dowsing. Good to see the old Atlantic in fighting mood. Was making six knots and more before I shortened sail last night. Wind dropped during the day and I am left with crazy, confused sea and a light breeze.

Weather today quite different from any other day. There is a white haze all around the horizon and much of the day the sun has been dulled as if in preparation for a storm. Have just sailed past a neon tube. Does this mean land is close?

Day 24 Latitude 18^0 57' Making a knot or two on 250

Perhaps

> Through this life I wander
> Watching all the time
> Checking with my inmost self
> Should this one be mine
>
> I don't want the make up
> Or silly pouting games
> Or giggling insignificance
> These birds are all the same.
>
> My search is for my woman
> A person whole and real
> A living loving adult
> Not merely sex appeal.
>
> Perhaps you are the one my love
> I would that it was so
> If we can find that this be true
> I'll never let you go.

Day 25 Immobilised right arm in a sling. My shoulder joint has been hurting, so will see if immobilisation helps. A veritable single hander. Now for a cold meatballs and oats breakfast. Am making my usual one knot. The Atlantic must love me, it is stringing this voyage out as long as possible.

Shoulder rather better today, though I am still resting it. Making 1-2 knots 260.

Have just read an article by P. Selznick 'Foundations of the theory of organisations' American Sociological review Vol 13 (1948) pp 25-35. It was the usual sociological drivel, oversimplified and superficial ideas expressed in complicated often meaningless prose.

Am just finishing reading 'Cancer Ward' for the second time. A truly marvellous book which illuminates the human condition with greater clarity and insight than sociologists will ever muster.

Have you ever thought of academic disciplines as an excuse for ignorance. Because I am a sociologist I can be ignorant of all other disciplines including history (political and economic), psychology, physiology, ethology, anthropology, archaeology etc. Rather than comprehending all that has been written about the human condition and seeking to add something new. The sociologist says – we ignore all of that and have a new and narrow way of looking at all phenomena. For the ancient Greeks, science, philosophy, art and politics were interwoven and combined into one worldview. We need more fabric and less strand.

Day 17 Latitude looks like 18^0 12' Gut is misbehaving so have stopped feeding it. Arm kept me awake last night so have stopped using it. Didn't feed gut for 22 hours, now when I feed it again it gets upset. Maybe it has had enough of oats and Gofio. I know I have.

Last evening there was a new kind of fish around the boat. This morning a new kind of bird. All white with a very long tail (frigate bird?). Frigate birds can fly for days on end so it is possible.

This stamp looks has the look.

Up to now there have only been a globular gliding gull and a tiny tit, dark brown with a white saddle. Makes me wonder if land is near. Don't really expect it for 2-4 weeks. If it arrives in less than two weeks, won't be far enough South to hit Barbados. All good antient navigators hit the right latitude early then run along it to their destination. Have considered broad reaching South for a few days and decided against it for the moment.

Latitude 17^0 41'   Dusk   Have just discovered that I caught something on my fishing line this afternoon. Don't know what, as he took my best hook and feather with him. Or the big thing that ate the little thing I caught did.

Day 28   Latitude 17^0 15'   Very little wind. Very little progress. Very hot sun. Emptied second collapsible waterbag yesterday. (maybe ten litres each)

Devised the flowchart for the perfect playing of NIM. If you want know about NIM then go to your Art House video shop and take out 'L'Annee Derniere a Marienbad' – Last Year at Marienbad. (Alternatively put the title into a web browser and you will get lots of references. It is even out on DVD.) It is a 60's black and white Nouvelle Vague - New Wave - flick. If they don't have it then it isn't a real Art House video shop.

Four weeks gone and all is well. Filling my spare moments by reading a wide range of material such as an article by Summerhof in the Penguin on Systems Thinking. It is very good. He is an analytical biologist who seeks to define mathematically the goal seeking behaviour of the higher living forms.

I used to believe that what distinguishes our species is that we can rise above fear and greed to indulge in play which has no material payoff. Well at least some of us can. Unfortunately, dogs, lions, jays and dolphins are also playful. We shall have to look elsewhere to justify our sense of superiority.

The 'look after number one', narcissistic, 'beggar thy neighbour', 'winning is everything' scum are a throwback to the era of the reptiles. Bring back the village, the tribe and the family. We advance through collaboration and co-operation. Well maybe competition helps a little. It is all a question of where you draw the amity - enmity boundary.

Dusk: Have just relieved my dietary monotony by cooking a pancake, biscuit, bread come damper out of baby's food. It is called Maizena. I thought that it might be something like Gofio. Didn't find out till I was under way that it was baby's food. It is very strange. Stirs like setting toffee, yet pours like milk. Another day shot to bits. One day this will end.

Day 29 Latitude 17⁰ 09' Light winds during the night. SW force one now. Am hanging to sea anchor. Lots of small debris in the water. Stuff like wood shaving (fibres), human (dolphin) excreta, foam from fishing floats etc. Have a small spider sprinting around on top of the water near the boat. All suggests that land is near except for the fact that the current runs from E to W. Either this stuff comes from ships or I am near the Cape Verde Islands.

The line which I tow along to grab should I happen to fall overboard has hundreds of crustaceans and other little creatures attached to it. As does Donna around the waterline. Pulled the rope out this morning to let the sun toast all these goodies away. Found a small crab on the line too. Now have him installed as king of my aquarium.

Steve Kopper quoted Euripides 'Those whom Gods would mock, they first make mad.'   I am feeling mocked by the Gods and am not happy about it.

Day 30 Half hour after dawn: Have just been checked out by a friendly eight foot shark and his pilot fish. Grabbed my trident to give him a prod, but he stayed out of reach. Often there are a group of Dorados following the shark around. Best place to ensure that you are not attacked by the shark is behind him.

Reminds me of the courtiers in human affairs, full of flattery, fashion and obsequience, playing to the powerful rather than making a contribution to greater understanding or improved performance. Most of the so called leaders in Australia are courtiers – little people, short of both courage and knowledge.

This afternoon brings up one calendar month I have been all at sea. Very light N wind during the night. Gusting zero now. Rain squall threatened last evening, had all sail down, rain collecting apparatus set up, all gear stowed and soap at the ready. Did it rain. Not on your Nelly.

Have decided that I am equally happy arriving in Antigua or Barbados. Will go whichever way the wind blows. Antigua is the safer target as it doesn't matter how far West I have come, I am on the right Latitude and by heading West will arrive. However I think that I am far enough away from the West Indies to head south to the Latitude of Barbados, then run it down.   Sailing directions for all of these islands are the same - drop around the Southern tip and enter the harbour.

Guy I met in Sete told me that he crossed in 28 days. Regular force 7 all the way. I have had no 7, no 6, no 5, very little 4, a touch of 3, some 2, some 1 and some calm. Doesn't look like a 28 day crossing does it. Besides this is the 30th day.

The lack of stimulus from another human being and the lack of any cues in my environment to establish my position lead to a high level of free floating anxiety. While it is probable that I am within 1000 miles of the West Indies I have no cues to confirm that belief. I have only ten more tins of oats.

The uncertainties of future life wash backwards and forwards through the mind. One day all things are possible. Next day it is not so clear. Today I am going to conduct my life along these lines, become a Senator or develop an automated factory. Tomorrow the script is quite different, write a novel or make a movie. As time goes on and one gets further from the real constraints of everyday life, these fantasies can grow into delicate, beautiful, towering, fragile bubbles in which one fervently believes for the day or hour of their incandescence.

I now find that those crustaceans I described yesterday are all over the under side of the boat. No wonder I don't make much progress. They must like my antifouling paint. Like some strawberry flavoured lipstick. Renewed the antifouling paint in the Balearics and in the Canaries it ought to be OK. I will not however be going over to scrape them off.

Nick Grainger in mid-Atlantic scraped many of the barnacles from the bottom of his boat. All the time scanning for sharks. Then he realised that the trail of barnacles arcing down into the deep was a trail that could be followed by a shark and that it lead to him. He abandoned the scrape and quickly clambered back into the boat.

There is a line in Grays Elegy which runs something like 'and all the world a quiet stillness holds', ('and all the air a solemn stillness holds' – ed). That's how it is out here except for the incessant gurgling of water surging in and out of the outboard well as the boat rises and falls.

Have just been reading Bombard's 'Nauffragé Voluntaire' (Shipwrecked voluntarily). At this time of year in about this position he had more than a week without wind. Nice to know that someone else knows how it feels! Alain Bombard, Nick Grainger and me. Well probably a few others as well.

Mid Afternoon Still very little wind. Have streamed sea anchor. That Shakespearian poem I couldn't think of the words to, runs something like this:

> What is love
> 'tis not hereafter
> present mirth
> hath present laughter
> In delay there lies no plenty
> So come and kiss me sweet and twenty
> Youth's a stuff will not endure.

Used to quote that once upon a time. Don't remember the title ... perhaps 'How about Now'.

Have two of those ferocious little hard skinned dorsal/ventral fin waving fishes under the boat. There were three this morning, but the third felt the barb of my trident and is no longer with us. The remaining two gaze at me reproachfully - with big black bulging eyes - from a safe distance.

Dusk: Just had a ship go by less than a mile away. Raised mainsail for him to see, put on kilt, got out whisky, water bottles, letter to post and pencil to write down position – did he stop – No sir. Am having a whisky anyway. Cheers.

If he was in the shipping lane to the East coast of South America, I am at approximately 17°N, 49° W. If it was the shipping lane to the Cape of Good Hope 17° N, 37° W. Would prefer it to be the former and if it is I am 660 miles from Barbados.

Just got a decent bearing on the setting sun 268. Gives a magnetic variation of 21°. If that is accurate I am crossing the New York - Cape of Good Hope shipping lane. But compass could be out 2°, bearing could be wrong 2°. The other shipping lane is only 2° different.

Day 31 Saw another ship. Donna has Dorados - maybe I will have fish for breakfast. Man 'the mighty hunter' strikes again.

Drove harpoon into lovely dorado about one hour before dawn. No bait. Just watched the way he swam around the boat and waited for him next time. Have just finished breckers. Was good. Will keep the meatballs till tomorrow.

Those ugly ferocious, foul smelling, thick skinned little fish are eating the crustaceans from the bottom of the boat. Sounds like a rat scratching in a locker, but it is only those ferocious little teeth cleaning Donna's bottom. The one I harpooned yesterday is back. He regards me with disapproval. Maybe they are eating their way through the bottom of the boat.

Latitude 16^0 58' Very light SW breeze. Hottest sun I have ever known. Too hot to be on deck. Have rigged canvas awning. Horrible little black fish are still eating those crustaceans. Don't think they will stop until they are all gone. Isn't that marvellous.

Quite a lot of large Dorados three ft plus around. Looks like fish breakfasts as long as this calm lasts. I take fish like medicine 'cause my body needs animal protein. Maybe if I had some oil, spices, rice and some fresh veggies I could cook something interesting.

Have just wounded my first shark. They annoy me the way they swim right up to touch my boat without the slightest fear. So .... gave the shark a good jab on the back and next time around beat him on the nose. If only I had an old style whaling lance, I reckon I could dispatch him with one good jab. His dignity hurt he slunk away. Can you have any dignity with a brain that small?

It was fascinating watching the dorados – about 20 of them up to four ft long – following the shark around to stay out of his line of attack. All happens very slowly. Sharks only seem to move at speed when striking.

Still no wind. Still extremely hot.

You may recall that I mentioned that there were fibres in the water – a sign of civilisation. I have just now realised that these fibres come from my own keel. I am grateful to my little black fishes for gobbling the crustaceans. However I hope that they leave sufficient keel for the boat to hold together.

Day 32   Force two E   Am under way again. Cold meatballs for breckers. Today's estimate says 1300 miles to go. That's another

20-30 days. A long time to continue on in this state of suspended animation. (It took another 27 days – Ed)

Hallelujah brother. Guess what. Mother nature took pity on me and sent a shower of rain. Collected some in a bucket and managed to get soaped up. This should be great I haven't washed in five weeks. So here I am all soaped up standing on deck waiting for the next shower of rain. It didn't come. I waited as long as I could then wiped the soap off with a towel. I feel great. The cleanest I have been for a very long time.

Day 34 Meandering along at half to one knot. Getting towards the tail end of a 24 hour fast. Yesterday made friends with a new breed of bird. Brown with white markings on the wings. Brown on the undercarriage too. Fed him some fish. He would fly down wind, circle round the boat and land in the water next to me. Am reading Shakespeare's King John and re-reading Decision at Delphi and The Rush that Never Ended. Time passes extraordinarily slowly.

Am fighting a losing battle with some little black flies. They like moist crannies and there are plenty on board. They breed like flies. I kill some every day, but not enough.

Day 35 Five weeks today! If this capricious mistress of mine does not stop messing me around, there is strong possibility of a desertion taking place. No wind last night. Poured with rain. But as sails were lowered they covered the rain collecting gear. So only got a pint.

This morning woke to the strongest wind I have had. Unbent square sails from the mast and stowed them securely. Stowed other loose gear and was ready to raise jib. By this time wind had weakened and shifted from NW to N. I could now therefore run under squares. Have got the squares out again and strung them in place with the usual round of untangling lines. Experienced yachties are familiar with the capricious wind, I was still learning.

Where am I

Imagine that you went five weeks without any feedback that what you were doing was taking you where you wanted to go. You start to doubt all of it, the operation of the sextant, the calculations, the nautical tables and the charts. Is it a conspiracy of cartographers? So I went back to first principles. Stepped through the geometry to prove to myself that my calculations were logical. Cannot see how the sextant can be far wrong. Fundamental problem is that one of these days I am going to run out of food. This produces anxiety and tension. Water will take a little longer, then ... goodnight. Lots of people do Christmas in the Canaries and then sail to take advantage of the more reliable winds. Maybe next time.

Latitude looks like 16^0 58' (not too accurate) Still making a quarter of a knot.

Day 36 Have just been visited by a pair of fish. Three or four feet long, skinny, brown with light coloured bands about two inches thick across the body. Always happy to see a cue that suggests I may be near land. Still rocketing along at half a knot. Too much cloud for a sun shot. Nice lot of rain, very refreshing. Unfortunately I am out of soap. Collected some water. Then calm all afternoon. Now at dusk have resumed my sedate half a knot. There are some fish around, but they are not volunteering for dinner.

This really is a beautiful, quiet, glorious scene. If I had more grub and knew my longitude, I might enjoy it rather more. Now all I want is to arrive.

Day 37 Becalmed as usual who needs land, water or food! Had some rain, a lunge at a Dorado (unsuccessful), a trim of beard (successful) and a quick sun shot. Latitude 16^0 03' N. Sails up and down a few times, never more than half a knot. Tomorrow I shall indulge my carnivorous preference with beef for breckers.

Monday was spent holding tiller from before dawn till after dusk. Lovely wind 4 gusting 5, unfortunately from the West! Reached South under jib, double reefed main and mizzen. Pity Barbados is to the West!

Day 39 Took off a couple of hours before dawn. Making 220 initially three knots now about one. Am watching Dorado and flying fish playing chasey. Dorados always chasing, often catching and devouring. Dorados try to fly and jump sometimes four feet in the air. Their pectoral fins are already well developed. Expect in the next million or two years they will evolve to a subspecies that can fly. The flying fish as they lose height dip the tip of their tail in the water, give few frenzied flourishes and fly some more. Dorado is in hot pursuit only inches away under the water ready to strike. Maybe observing this contest contributed to Darwin's insight into the survival of the fittest.

To address my cramps, have had a cup of sea water on each of the last two days. Tastes OK and doesn't seem to do any harm. Shall continue the practice. Should hit the 13th parallel this weekend. Will run along it on tippy toe till I hit Barbados. Can't be soon enough.

Woken by shark bumping bottom. He was about eight feet long and took no notice of my first few jabs with the trident. Then I got one in a few inches behind the nose. He was softer than I expected and only just managed to get the trident out before his great body disappeared with a wild swish of the tail. Peace again reigneth.

Day 40 Half an hour after dawn. Another or the same shark in a bit of a frenzy making passes under the boat and bumping quite hard. Something under there was edible. Couldn't get near him with my knife so gave him a couple of jabs with trident and off he went.

The tin of oats I opened yesterday had lots of mould in it. All of the others smell mouldy. Am giving them some air, hoping that will improve matters. I can't afford to throw away food.

My shark just came back for a return visit. Didn't stay long. The problem for sharks when fishes press themselves to the bottom of Donna is how to get a mouthful. The shark has large fairly rigid pectoral fins which give him great manoeuvrability when there is plenty of water around. However his mouth is below and behind his snout. Therefore he has to roll on his side or even further over to bite fish which are pressed to the underside of my boat.

When he does this near the boat, the pectoral fin hits the edge of the boat and deflects him. Must be very frustrating.

The most annoying thing about sharks is that they are so absolutely sure of themselves. Is smallness of brain correlated with attitude? We on the other hand are born with inferior hardware and lots of brain. So we make weapons to even the odds. I need a whaling lance.

Not having any wind brings on a crescendo of anxiety about ever reaching land. It got so bad this morning that I was unable to read or think about anything else. So I reviewed my situation. I have enough food for at least another 30 days. If I haven't arrived by then I wasn't meant to and might as well RIP. I could last longer, but will worry about that if necessary. The relative calm I am now experiencing comes from making specific and definite plans for the next 30 days.

I have six tins of oats (two with mould I think). I shall consume them two per week. I have two kilos of Gofio and a dozen small tins of sardines. A vitamin pill every second day should make them last. Three and a half large tins of dried milk (one per week). Some liferaft rations – one tin of biscuits, one packet with 12 small vitamin impregnated cubes of bread and eight cubes of glucose. Will try to save these till I am desperate. Have enough water for six weeks – I think.

Amusingly, one of my ways of coping with anxiety under normal circumstances is to eat rather more than usual. Oral gratification and all that. Shall have to find a new way. Still no wind.

Latitude 14^0 24' N No wind. Forty days and forty nights have I sat in, scrambled over, nursed and driven this little boat and to what end? Still there is this circle of blue around me and I don't know where I am.

Day 41 One hour after dawn. Reaching South under force 1 Easterly. Last evening, return visit by shark. Banged him in the eye. He turned in his own length and disappeared. Think I have been underestimating the length of these sharks. This one was half the length of the boat. Let's say a ten footer. Later in the night two sharks in feeding frenzy ten metres from the boat. Some blood in the water certainly gets them going.

Today am drinking collected rain water. It is greasy from the canvas and has mould or fungus from the can. Boiled it but it still tasted awful. Making 2-3 knots on 220. When I am under way like this I spend my time thinking about arriving seeing friends, collecting mail etc. I prefer this to thinking about not arriving.

Latitude 14⁰ 11' N Mid Afternoon: Making 1-3 knots 220 Have just discovered that one large jerry can of water is growing a bright green sickly looking mould. The jerry can was a gift and used to carry poisonous chemicals. My oily rain water has just moved one notch up the pecking order.

Day 42 Did a foolish thing last night. Tried to sail all night. I want to get to the Latitude of Barbados. But I am stretched too thin to go without sleep as well. Began making mistakes. Have now lost my plastic bucket and nearly broke the tiller. I placed the bucket in the outboard well to stop it falling overboard. It didn't fall overboard, it fell straight down the well and away.

I stupidly forced the tiller when trying to reverse the rudder before pulling it out. It was simply a question of doing things in the right order. Usually I take down the sails, then take out the tiller. This time I did it the other way around and now the tiller rudder connection is very week. The wood is split and the bolt bent.

Still I made good headway. Proper fast dingy sailing much of the night. Also an unwarranted risk methinks. Capsize and you're dead. Was exciting though. All one has to do as a single hander is do things in the wrong order and you are in big trouble.

Latitude looks like 13⁰ 13' N The advantage of sailing through the night was getting to this Latitude now rather than midday tomorrow. Now I just have to run West to Barbados. Am setting the squares.

Wind has lessened, but am slowly heading West. Don't expect Barbados to come over the horizon for some time, but am sitting on deck looking West anyway.

Would like however:
- ❑ 2 avocado vinaigrette
- ❑ 1 large pea soup with sippets
- ❑ 1 plate of small savoury sausages 'cevapcici' a la Vineyard Charcoal Grill, Acland Street, St Kilda

- ❑ 1 thick large rare fillet with champignons and broccoli
- ❑ 1 side salad with French dressing
- ❑ 1 huge plate of fruit salad with cream and ice cream
- ❑ many cups of strong dark coffee
- ❑ box of big fat cigars
- ❑ 1 bottle of Napoleon brandy
- ❑ 1 big bed to sleep it off in.

Even the idiotic Mediterranean would be impressed by the Atlantic's current effort.

- ❑ Large long fast old swell from N
- ❑ Medium steep fast swell from S
- ❑ Medium plus chop plus wind from the East
- ❑ Medium size and speed from the SE.

Lovely, bobbing, jumping, dancing sea. Wind is shifting to the NE so that should make it better still. Just cut the top off a jerry can so I can use it as a 'jerry'. Who needs a plastic bucket.

Last night saw a satellite, the first piece of man's handiwork I have seen for some time. Also last evening a new variety of bird. Black, red face, white beak, small body, big batlike wings, and two long skinny tail feathers or legs. Does this indicate that land is near?

Day 43 Heaven must be somewhere where you can drink as much water as you like. Making a knot between 270 and 300. There are dark clouds on the horizon West of me all the time. Keep watching them waiting for that upper edge to sharpen indicating land. Hasn't happened yet.

'Mount Hilaby on Barbados, 1115 feet with conical hills to the North East called Scotland' says the reference in the Pilot. I even have the vertical sextant angle required to keep me off the reef on South Point - 40 minutes on lighthouse plus 18' index error pretty close to 1^0. We will see if there is time for sextant play when approaching land.

Latitude 12^0 59' Just saw three lovely little tropical fishes seven inches long, brown with large white dots. Long pectoral fin with trailing tendrils. Perhaps I am headed in the right direction.

Day 44 Did battle last night for an hour with a firm large stool. Was terrified of busting a blood vessel or the sphincter, but all seems in order. Hung to sea anchor for some hours last night and had a proper sleep. My hands and legs both had the shakes. Set two squares shortly after midnight. Will now set brown sails and make some Northing.

Saw a seagull this morning. Definitely a land bird, large body and small skinny wings compared to the ocean birds.

Have decided to:
- lose as little Northing as possible overnight
- get a good nights sleep
- to continue NW in the morning.

Forty four days and I am feeling the accumulated weariness. Inadequate diet, not enough sleep and high levels of anxiety leave me feeling a bit run down. Wind capricious today – much sail changing (too much). The Atlantic might as well give in and carry me to Barbados as I shall sit here like a zombie making headway in the right direction forever if necessary. Continue to look forward to a feed, a little romance and some chat with friends. Kerstin where are you?

One hour before sunset Just been on the edge of a line squall. Raining over there, but not here. Strong wind, so got sails off her and sea anchor out. Am now waiting to see what happens next. Being caught with too much sail up could lead to capsize which would not be convenient.

Day 45 Am operating at a very low level, every action an effort. Gums are bleeding, so am back on one vitamin pill per day. They will run out, but what the hell, at least I will postpone the bleeding for a while.

Got a bearing on the setting sun last night 18^0 variation. Means 700 miles to go. Wasn't very accurate, so don't know. Might arrive tomorrow (very doubtful) or may not be there for 3-4 weeks. (It took two weeks - Ed)

You may recall in week two I said I would stay to the North so as not to have problems with NE wind after arriving at the Latitude of Barbados. I am now on that Latitude and cannot use my square sails as the wind has too much North in it and is too strong. The irony of it is that for 44 days I have wanted strong

NE winds and haven't had them. Now when I cannot run before them they have arrived.

Sea anchor last night and sea anchor now to get this bearing straight and to cook meatballs. Am getting worn down, but I think that there is quite a way to go before I become dysfunctional. I have become methodical and systematically do all the things that must be done – navigating, sail handling and cooking. I sleep in my little locker starkers with a fragment of lightweight sleeping bag across my chest. I daresay it would make sense to have a mattress of some sort. Still the current system has worked OK to here.

These sights did not seem right so I listed them.
- Thursday 14^0 11'
- Friday 13^0 13'
- Saturday 12^0 59'
- Sunday   ---
- Monday 13^0 49'
- Tuesday 13^0 49'

These readings seem to vary more than makes sense. Have just checked the declination from the table and the sums. Not able to check the sights. Must get on the right Latitude or I will miss Barbados. Have set three squares and am running West. Am worried sick. Feel much as I did when I was about to be run down that first night out from Las Palmas. Something is badly wrong and I am unable to understand.

There is sometimes a strong Northerly current this side of Barbados. But I don't think I am that close. However – one knot of Northerly current for a couple of days could account for the change between Saturday and Monday. All these sights were taken under difficult conditions – so all are subject to error. What is so frightening is that I rely on that noon sight to guide me to Barbados.

My logic is as follows:
- If a current has taken me North and I am close to Barbados then by proceeding West I should see the light on Harrison Point, should I happen to get there tonight.
- If I am further from Barbados, then I will get a sight at tomorrow noon and see what it says.

In this last week I have spent some days going first South, then North. It is time I went West. I have been hungry and thirsty long enough. Am considering running full speed under whatever wind comes. Would rather the boat was broken on the South American coast than me starve while playing fancy navigation games out here. The last two nights I have had lovely strong NE winds and have spent them hanging to the sea anchor! Have just looked at the Pilot books for Grenada, Tobago and Trinidad. Will see what tomorrow brings.

Day 46 Some strong wind during the night. Ended up on the sea anchor again. Had quite a lot of rain one hour after sunrise. Collected half a bucket of water, looks dirty, tastes greasy but it is WATER.

Ship just passed about a quarter of a mile away. Considered firing smoke flare (a la Fairfax) or flashing at the bridge with a mirror (a la Bombard). Rejected both. Would love them to have come across and given me an accurate position and some food and water. However I got myself into this mess. Now I shall get myself out. Sunny day, low rounded waves very pleasant. I kept watching this ship as it slowly went past and eventually disappeared. I have need of some conversation.

Making one knot on 290. Very interested to see that noon day Latitude. Sighted another long tailed, skinny winged - flapping rather than gliding - land based gull. Latitude 13^0 49' Bloody boat is jumping about like a dervish. I can tolerate the pitching and the oh so tender rolling, but the yawing makes taking a sight extraordinarily difficult.

No longer am I trying to claw my way North, but am allowing a little South with lots of West. Mount Hilaby (13^0 17' N) visible from 30 miles should be within my North to South range by this time tomorrow. As I doubt very much that I have passed Barbados, I shall drop South to 13^0 30' and try to hold it there.

I have just seen another ship. The same design as this mornings on the same sort of course. It seems that I am in a shipping lane of some sort. It is not marked on my charts. Both had central bridge, stern mounted funnel and accommodation. No other superstructure. Unable to translate these sightings into navigational data.

Day 47   Good morning folks.   Life is beaut out here.   Have collected some more rain water. Am even saving the water which collects in the cockpit bilge. It is very dirty, but I prefer it to my green slime, poisonous chemical brew. Come to think of it I am not going to drink this green water. I might as well throw the jerry can overboard, it is just useless weight. Just did. Watched it float away.

In one of the yachtie books I have read, the author spoke of throwing a can of fresh water overboard and watching it sink. Problem is that cans of fresh water don't sink in salt water. This inaccuracy cast doubt on everything else in the book.

New thought: I wonder if those ships were on the shipping route passing N of Venezuela in the Caribbean. ie. could I have sailed past the West Indies already? I doubt it, but who knows.

This lovely little boat. It makes 40^0 difference to my course when I shift from one side of the cockpit to the other. Just had enormous trouble passing stools again. Has happened each day for the last few. There were some traces of blood today – am rupturing something. Will have to change my diet a little. Too much dried milk and dry oats and not enough water. Will fast for a day to sort things out first.

One knot on 290   Cannot understand why, but today I feel in excellent spirits. My body is moving better than it has for weeks. Perhaps the Maizena or the sugar and cocoa contain something lacking in my normal diet. Perhaps the grease from my water collecting canvas is really a tonic.   More likely yesterday's meatballs have provided some real nourishment for a change. Maybe I should drink a little more water.

Latitude 13^0 50'   Knees worn crawling about on prickly home made fibreglass locker top. Have just designed what is known as a cybernetics factory – fully automated. It is to produce objects similar to circular slide rules. Rotating discs with different scales on each. The first such product will be a new musical notation I have invented for finding chords on any musical instrument. It uses twelve equal semitone intervals, rather than eight intervals some of which are tones and some semitones. Does that sound OK?

Have been making a quarter of a knot since midday. Have just re-read the pilot about wind and weather in this region. Trade winds are most reliable in January, February and March. It will soon be January! Also calculated on the chart what happens if I am already past the West Indies. In something less than 30 days I should hit Central America. However before that I should see many ships heading for the Panama Canal. What is the appropriate strategy? Get as far West as possible as soon as possible.

Have also read the Pilot on St Vincent and St Lucia. Am not going to head South to 13^0 30' will stay on this Latitude until driven South. Am quite happy to make a landfall on St Vincent or St Lucia. Both have nice tall mountains higher than 3000 ft. Somehow today I have the feeling that everything will be OK.

Day 48 Making 1-2 knots 270 Neither ship nor land on the horizon. Had a pre dawn snack of sardines smashed in Gofio. Opened new tin of oats. There are now three left. They are fresh and delightful. Have been eating the mould flavoured tin for five days (helped to make it last). C'est la vie.

Latitude 13^0 54' Maybe a bit further South. Had rain and cloud interrupting sights. My gull visited me last night, just before sunset and is here again now. Wish I could talk to the blighter. He knows where we are. Or is he just doing his thing and it doesn't matter where we are? A bit like me really.

Sunset: Have just decanted some of my oily water. Man its oily. Looks like I have carried another large jerry can of water all this way for nothing. Have one week of good water left. Don't think that will be enough.

Day 49 Seven weeks today. Dawn. My gull has just come to visit me again. Surely he must be a good omen. Organised a jerry built jerry seat. Managed to crap without cutting my backsides or anything else on the plastic edge. Can't be too careful.

Latitude 13^0 46' Have been doing a bit of reading today. Mary Blewitt – Celestial Navigation. Should I venture out to sea again I will make sure that I am equipped for compleat navigation. The Vinland Sagas – would still like to sail the Viking route to America. Emery and Trist – The causal texture of organisational environments, Human Relations Vol 18 (1965) pp 21-32. An article which says that economists, sociologists and biologists ought to face up to the complexity of the environments they study. Not before time. Captain Derham – Cruising the Aegean Royal Cruising Club. Informed but not exciting. And the West Indies Pilot of course. Have examined the sailing directions for all of the islands where I might make a landfall. Bring it on. I am ready.

Have got the gobbles, my 'won't power' has given out on me. You wouldn't think that oats could still taste good after all this time. Am trying the oily water too. Would be a shame to go of lead poisoning.

Day 50 Dawn – three gulls this morning. Am toying with the idea of heading South to the Latitude of Barbados. Might mean a landfall 2-3 days sooner. That would be good.

Was within 1 degree of the noon day sight when big black cloud and strong South - YES SOUTH - wind arrived. Clung on with jib and full main expecting it to last only a few minutes. It lasted close to an hour. Was spilling most of the wind out of both sails most of the time. Now have a gentle SE breeze.

Have been in a curious state these last few days. Like a candle which gives a last sparkle before it dies. I feel good and move well, but don't want to sleep. Like a man with only a few hours left to live. Yet I can survive at least three weeks, probably more than a month and surely I will have made a landfall by then.

My gull just came back and flew all around. What I need is that old Viking trick of releasing a crow and watching which way it flies to find land. Seem to run OK on SAE 90 – oily water. Maybe it will lubricate my bowel.

Day 51 Wish I could count the days in (n-x) mode ie. days to go. Mid morning: Spent much of last night sitting by the tiller on the brink of taking control or dropping the sails. However Donna managed. Four and Five knots for hours. Thrown about like mad, but what the hell.

Am sleepy and irritable this morning. Have cooked all and devoured half of my last tin of meat. Ye olde meatballs. Strange to say there doesn't seem to be any land in sight yet. Am running a few degrees South of downwind on 260. Wind last night was almost as strong as everyone told me I would get continuously. If I had had that I might have crossed in 30 days. However that would have denied me this last three weeks of pleasure.

Latitude 13^0 04' This implies that I have come 40 miles South in 48 hours. During 12 of those hours I sailed South at speeds between one and three knots. For the rest courses S of W by varying amounts at speeds ranging from half a knot to five knots. In case of doubt head West. Intractable problems usually trigger conservative strategies.

Had the brown sails up for a while. They didn't improve velocity so am back with the greens. Light winds all afternoon. Barbados is still hiding over the horizon somewhere. Opened the second last tin of oats. Times will start getting grim shortly.

Day 52 Last night wind from the NE and freshening and me very tired, so hung on as long as I could stay awake, then sea anchor. Up at dawn running with three squares set low. Good strength of wind, but am heading too far South. My gull is circling around seems to want to land on the mast.

Wind is weak and useless now. I am trying to sail 280 at one knot. Have just spent a long day holding the tiller. Dingy sailors normally race for an hour or two. Holding the tiller and paying attention to steering over every wave for twelve hours leaves one feeling a little weary.

Christmas Eve

Have stopped trying to believe that Barbados will pop up over the horizon tomorrow and instituted severe rationing. My dinner was two spoonfulls of oats. Haven't had a drink all day. Took many waves over the stern and was nearly rolled a couple of times. Am wet but content. Tomorrow I will make some more miles West.

Day 53 Away a couple of hours before dawn with two squares. Later full set of browns until dusk. Two to six knots all day. Best day since Las Palmas. Breakfast one inch square cube of vitamin impregnated bread. Lunch two Polish life boat biscuits. Dinner two Polish life boat biscuits. Tasted heavenly. Latitude something S of 13^0 23'. Shot was terminated by a large wave joining in. Good to make some progress for a change. Who needs food. Merry Christmas all.

Day 54 Twilight Sitting here waiting for some dark wet clouds to pass. Wondering whether to set squares and let her run for the night. At present hanging to sea anchor. A good day. Broad reach all brown. Nearly pitchpoled once, nearly rolled twice, sprinkled many times and inundated once. They say that an anxious man with a bucket is the fastest way to shift a lot of water. They are right. Had one come in green. Shifted it out again as quickly as possible. Rather frightening really.

Inadvertent gybe once. Nearly rolled several more times. Really too much wind for me. These conditions are what everyone describes as Trades. Should have been having this since the beginning.

Day 55 This morning spent some hours considering the situation before raising the jib and heading off on a run 265. Was making good speed and having less trouble than the day before.

Your friend and humble narrator has just looked death right in the eye. Eyeball to eyeball. 'tis only the Gods that preserve me. Donna was picked up by a larger than normal wave and accelerated straight down the front at a very steep angle. The nose went under, water rushing in green over both sides. I thought that was me done for as the wave was still pushing Donna down. However it got worse. We began to broach and the port gunwale went under for the length of the boat. I know not how or why but Donna struggled out from under all of this and was still floating, full of water when the wave had gone.

I have emptied out the bulk of the water and had a feed. There seems little point in heavy rationing if I may not be here to eat the goodies.

There is a continuing danger of a large wave doing us in. Need to keep the nose pointing at the waves to diminish the chance of being rolled. Tried lying to the sea anchor, the rope pulled too strongly and we went from lying across the sea this way to lying across the sea that. Also the pull on the rope was so strong that the rope started to strand and there seemed to be a risk of being pulled through a wave.

Tried streaming a long loop of rope from the bow. Not enough drag to keep the nose into the wind and seas. Tried trailing a sail – supposed to get the wave to break early before the boat. The wave effect didn't matter because the sail didn't keep the nose into the sea. Tried a transverse spar on the end of a line. There was enough pull to keep the nose into the wind. We were being pushed downwind. Didn't want to lose ground, but the first problem was to survive this little blow.

Didn't get to take a sight. The waves were bigger than 20 ft and I felt that I must sit and watch and be ready to bail. That night, I hardly slept. What sleep I did get was crumpled in the cockpit. Hatch was lashed shut. I was willing Donna to get up and over each wave.

Webb Chiles on his Pacific voyage in a Drascombe Lugger found that when swamped he could not bail the water out faster than it was coming in through the centreplate housing. This meant that his boat stayed full of water till it smashed on the reef. My extra locker in the mid section of the boat kept the water away from the centreplate housing. This meant that the boat floated higher and I was able to get the water out of the other sections of the boat and stay buoyant. It saved my life.

Day 57   There is no record in the log for Friday. The day was spent getting over the waves one by one.

Yachties would call yesterday's wave a freak wave. While it was freaky it is actually a normal consequence of intersecting wave trains. Sometimes they get in phase and create a high wave face and a deep hole – get an engineer to explain it to you. Tankers have been broken in half off Durban by this phenomenon. The question of fate is that you happen to be at this particular place at this particular time.

Day 58   Conditions have moderated so set sail under jib and mizzen 300, 20^0 leeway 1-2 knots. Found that jib has large tear near reefing eyelet. Am using it anyway will fix tonight. Last night had full night's sleep and woke very seedy. Spent the morning thinking and moving very slowly. Stomach and some other parts wanted to cramp.

Wonderful what a mouthful of oats will do to an underfed man. Had same late morning. Came alive (relatively) Took sight - Latitude looks like 13^0 01' N - and here I am, still in the middle of nowhere but making progress again.

A day of successive squalls bearing down on me with quite strong winds. Sailed under jib and mizzen all day often making six knots. In the morning while doing three knots in rough sea with one leg over the tiller, harpooned a three ft Dorado and brought him on board. This pleased me for three reasons:
- something to eat (I could last a while longer)
- it showed that my reflexes had not completely deserted me
- it showed that the Gods were still on my side (most important)

Cooked some Dorado late afternoon. It was great. Cut thin small pieces and toasted them in the hot frying pan. Stove kept going out. Largely because it had been under water several times and was running on a mixture of kero and salt water. Resolved to cook the rest of the Dorado in the morning.

Day 59 Prepared breakfast inside the locker with closed lid. Did a few jobs on deck, then thought that I noticed something on the horizon. Put on glasses and looked again. It was still there. Cleaned glasses and saw LAND.

Now I had been scanning the horizon all round the boat for 59 days. Often there were clouds which might have been land. This time the upper edge stayed solid. Finally I had made a landfall. However I didn't go into a state of jubilation. This is not a soccer match on the TV with lots of punching the air for the cameras. What I did was remember that most skiing accidents happen on the last run of the day, when you relax and take it easy. I was telling myself to pay attention. It was still too far to swim.

Thought that it was probably Barbados, but could not be sure. Could see a lighthouse which could be Kittridge point. I saw a fishing boat. Sailed up close enough to hail them. Asked them what island it was. 'Barbados' they said. I must confess to being a trifle chuffed at having hit my intended destination.

I sailed on taking it very carefully, staying well clear of the point. Didn't use the sextant, I could see the bottom anyway. Running aground on the point would be really silly.

It was mid afternoon by the time I sailed around the southern tip of the island and reached across Carlisle Bay. Tacked and tried to get up the wind into the bay. A brisk wind blowing (maybe 4) I had jib and mizzen up. Tacked again and tried harder to get in towards the shore. I was not making much progress. Tacked again.

I had been at sea for 59 days and had found Barbados. I just wanted to walk on the land. Sailed onto the sand spit on the Southern side of the bay, jumped out and stood on the land. The water was about a foot deep. It was a bombora. The waves were three feet high. The centreplate is bashing on the sand. Reached in and pulled up the centreboard. Walking in the shallows, I started to tow the boat round towards the harbour. Some friendly people in a little yellow water ski boat offered to tow me in.

A moment to consider what an ignominious end to my voyage this would be, before gratefully accepting.

Barbados

Anchored in the midst of the other yachts. There were more than fifty. Some English friends Nick and Julie Grainger came alongside with bread, fresh limes. Very thoughtful. They had crossed in 'The Aegre', a 21ft decked in Shetland whaler (more correctly a Fourern).

This photograph was taken by Nick Grainger shortly after my arrival in Carlisle Bay off Bridgetown Barbados.
The guest is an American - Gordon Yates.

Searched for my yellow quarantine flag. I could not find it. For those of you who don't know, the convention is that you fly the yellow quarantine flag and no one comes near you until you have been cleared by customs. What was I to do. I sat and waited. However the customs people were unlikely to find me with no yellow flag. In fact they would not know I was there.

So I swam ashore to the yacht club and asked their advice. They said 'first get back on your boat and we will call them'. A long time later the customs boat appeared and the officer expressed considerable displeasure with the fact that I had been ashore. However in due course when I had filled out the same large forms that a visiting ocean going liner would use, we had everything in order and I was cleared. We shared a glass of whisky. My first agreeable interaction with a Bajan.

Went ashore and into the first office I found. 'May I use your phone?' Made a reverse charge call to Australia to advise my family that I had arrived. They were a little surprised to hear from me as they had decided that I had gone to the bottom. They had been put on edge by a telephone call from US suggesting that I was long overdue. However, I had written to them from the Canaries saying that I thought it would take somewhere between 30 and 60 days. Seems to me that 59 is less than 60.

That night I was entertained by Jan-Olof on Costa Mera with delightful dinner of Swedish salt herring, potatoes, and vodka. The third member of the dinner party was an Englishman who did not enjoy the salt herring or the vodka. His only comment was that the potatoes were delightful.

Charlie Hughes on British Trimaran

Next day a fellow yachtie took me shopping to the wholesale supermarket. I bought lots of stuff – four big boxes. We stopped for a quick rum and coke on the way back to the yacht club. Then we had another. We emerged - barely able to walk - in the early hours. During this evening I discovered the 'bump'. A strange dance with lots of bumping hips and things. We eventually got back to the yacht club and found the gate locked. No worries we will get in via the beach. Well the tide was in and the sea wall extended out a fair way out into the water. However we were feeling no pain and made our way around the wall with boxes on our shoulders and the water lapping high on the chest.

We got the stuff into a borrowed dingy and rowed out towards my boat. I was rowing. Couldn't work out why the dingy was filling up with water. We were sinking, so I headed for Costa Mera. We woke Jan-Olof up and went on board. Left the dingy tied up to Costa Mera and swam back to my boat. Unfortunately my provisions were floating in the dingy overnight and most of them had to be discarded. Still I learned to dance the 'bump'.

That night all the English speakers in the harbour were invited to a New Year's eve party on board a beautiful wooden Colin Archer double ender. These boats were derived from the pilot boats that kept station in the rough seas off the Norwegian coast. Splendid very seaworthy boats. There was a large number of people on board, seemed like hundreds. These were lovely people. Mainly yachties who had crossed the Atlantic.

Normally I would have enjoyed speaking with – partying with – this crowd. However, we were pressed together like sardines. I had been completely alone for two months and could not stand having so many people so close. I jumped overboard and swam back to lovely little Donna.

The owners of the Colin Archer were a retired English dentist and doctor. Whenever the bacon and eggs didn't taste new and fresh, they would sail on to another destination. These were true 'cruising' people.

Christmas party aboard the 'Aegre'

I had missed the Christmas Party with Nick and Julie aboard Aegre. How do you throw a party for 25 people aboard a 21 foot yacht?

I had lunch with Nick on Easter Sunday 2005. Very interesting to discuss the voyage with someone who knew what it was like. He started one day ahead of me from Tenerife and arrived two weeks before me in Barbados. He had a keel, a cabin and an accomplice, also he had been sailing the same craft in an Outward Bound school in Scotland for some time, so he knew the boat. Nick and Julie made a spectacular voyage ending in a dismasting during a storm in the strangely named Pacific. It took them two weeks to reach land.

New years Day. The sun is shining and I am happily enjoying the scene in Carlisle Bay. The crisis of a few days ago doesn't seem very relevant now. We found a little cafe in the cheap end of town that served Bajan stew, three small pieces of meat, a mound of rice, lots of gravy, some black eyed beans and a little salad $2.50 BB less than $1 Australian. Similar to peasant fare in many countries, rice or noodles for bulk with a little meat for flavouring. We were there for lunch almost every day.

Spent several weeks in Carlisle Bay. Two English and I would foregather on the beach on the dot of ten AM every morning for a game of beach cricket. Every Barbadian who went past would have a bat and a bowl. No English stonewalling here. These guys wanted to hit a six on every ball and bowl you out first ball. Now Aussie and English blokes are not renowned for romantic insight, however we formed the impression that there was a smidge of interest from passing Bajan beauties.

Met some Canadian, American and English tourists at a condominium complex. The celebrity was Jimmy Edwards. Jimmy, his handsome friend and I were invited in to lunch. Jimmy was in jovial good form. It was the best feed I had had in a very long time.

Met a retired American who wanted to help the locals become self sufficient in food production. Barbados was covered in sugar plantations, but did not grow local fruit or vegetables. Almost all the food came in by ship. He set up a grapefruit farm, but could not get the locals to take it seriously and eventually abandoned the project.

However the locals were happy, especially when the West Indies captured a wicket in a test match. They all had transistor radios glued to their ears and jumped about in celebration. The other reason they were happy is that they were the first island to be granted independence. I found much stronger resentment of 'whitey' in Jamaica.

A little story about French and English naval rivalry in the Caribbean. The Brits occupied Barbados. The French fleet came across the Atlantic each season to capture Barbados. They would try for Barbados, lose the battle, then head downwind to St Lucia and take that instead.

Being French they may have just bypassed Barbados and headed for St Lucia to party. The early French scientific expeditions to Australia spent minimum time on research before heading off for the delights of Polynesia. A certain 'savoir vivre'. When the French fleet moved on the English would come and take back St Lucia. St Lucia changed hands 16 times.

An Article from the Daily Telegraph of 29 April 1973

Before the voyage I had set up a running news story in newspapers in Australia and the UK. When I arrived in Barbados it seemed irrelevant. Making the voyage was enough. I was very happy to be alive.

I spent several very pleasant weeks in Barbados, but couldn't stay forever? I had thought of sailing back to Australia. However my recent experiences had led me to the view that there was significant risk in this sailing lark. Then I got some news from St Vincent.

St Vincent

St Vincent is 80 miles West of Barbados. Slaves would escape from Barbados by clinging to a log and floating West on the current. Many of these ex slaves stayed free leavening the atmosphere on St Vincent.

St Vincent anchorage

I heard on the grapevine that Costa Mera was in St Vincent, so I too headed West. Found Jan-Olof with his wife and two kids Johan and Lotta aged nine and ten. They had been cruising the Grenadines - a magical uninhabited archipelago. He accepted a job as skipper of a cruise yacht for a few months before heading back to Sweden and his old boring job as a teacher of teachers. However he found having been at sea for two years and met a very wide range of people that life in middle class conformist Sweden was stultifying.

Met an English couple on Red Martlett with daughters aged four and five. They had decided to abandon conformist, materialist, high density city living and take to the seas. He missed the Sunday lunches with lace tablecloth and mother. She thought that it was great to be able to throw the scraps over the side and not have to clean the house. I looked after their kids a couple of times while they went out to party. Let me know if you have heard of them.

As always people introduced themselves to me. One guy was very drunk. I found that he had been drunk for a week. His story was that his wife had tried to shoot him. Her story was that he had tried to shoot her, but she had got the gun and escaped onto a cruising yacht. These two published the local English language glossy magazine. They were not speaking and the business was in trouble. He found that I had been a management consultant and asked if I would run the publishing business. I said yes.

Next day we flew to St Lucia. We were selling advertising space in the coming issue, collecting outstanding debts and chasing the printer in Trinidad about the next edition. That night I went out drinking with a local. He was in the police reserve (so he said) and carried a hand gun. We were roaming from bar to bar. I found it boring and got out of the car and walked away. He began shooting into the ground either side of me as I walked across a park. Fortunately he did not drill me in the back.

Each island has a few families who are in control of things. Met the patriarch of one of these, a Caribbean Medici. The family ran the local newspaper, a book shop and more. He was interested in ownership of the magazine. He offered me a consulting assignment to improve the operation of the newspaper. This would get me out of the way so that he could acquire the magazine. I was interested, but non committal. After all, at this particular moment, I was the publisher.

Then the distaff half of the publishing duo came back and my involvement with the magazine was over. However, I did get paid for my weeks work.

Back on St Vincent I suggested half in jest to a friend that we get a sheep and have a barbeque. At eight AM next morning he banged on my boat to wake me saying 'get your knife I have the sheep'. Some Scots had migrated to the St. Vincent about one hundred years prior. They lived in the hills in a primitive subsistence time warp. They were dismissed by the locals as 'poor white trash'. Their livestock ran by the road. They were now one sheep down.

Now I had observed my brother despatching a sheep, but had never actually done it myself. However this was the moment. There was a crowd of about ten people watching. I stepped up grasped the sheep, pulled it to a vertical position and applied the knife to the throat. Rather like playing a cello. The locals usually stabbed down the side of the throat and got the heart leading to a rapid death. It became clear that they knew lots more about this than me. I handed the knife to them. The first thing they did was remove the testicles and ran off to cook and eat them. Something about doubling the prowess.

That night we had a 'boil in'. This is everything you have got in the house, including half the sheep, plus some curry into a soupy casserole. Of course we had a party to go with the casserole. It was an outstanding night. The hostess was a beautiful melange of several racial sources including something from Europe and something from Asia. Her partner was a Swedish surgeon who had come to St Vincent to avoid the severe Swedish income tax. He was an entrepreneur. When the flour ran out on any island, his small trading ship would appear and sell flour direct to the punters on the dock. It was a long way from being the 'caring surgeon'.

The day after the party I played a round of golf with the hostess and a friend of hers. New beautiful, tropical golf course. Fairways seemed to narrow where the drive was landing. Couldn't quite see why this was a good idea. I was a bit out of touch anyway. I hadn't played in bare feet since I was 10 years old.

I decided to sail up to St Lucia and see about this consulting assignment. In very light winds ghosted up the leeward coast of St Vincent. There were stories about yachts being plundered and sunk so I really wanted to get across the strait to St Lucia as soon as possible. Making very slow progress.

A siren (young damsel) beckoned from a small inlet. Now I know the stories about yachts being lured onto the rocks by sirens – was it Ulysses that was tied to the mast? However I am a sailor. I alter course and head for the inlet.

When I get there she has vanished. There is a trail winding up the escarpment. Late afternoon I reach a small village. They bring the two young Americans who are there on a volunteers abroad project to meet me. I am sent to buy some beer.

There are no shops in this village. However one of the locals keeps a little extra beer for such occasions. I go to his place. This house is very basic - no internal lining on the walls. However the walls are decorated with extensive chalk writing which records the scores from the test matches over the last three years. Clearly this is a man's house and he cares about cricket.

This caused me to think what a load of wimps the males in the West are. In a traditional American, English or Australian family the bloke funds the purchase of the house which is then set up for the pleasure of the wife. The front room has the good furniture and is established in case the Queen, the bride's mother or the mother in law come to visit. Its a chick thing. The bloke does not feel at home here and the children are not allowed into these rooms. The bloke knows that his place is the shed at the bottom of the garden, the pub or the doghouse.

So we have a beer and a chat till late evening. These American volunteers abroad are teaching English and perhaps learning a little about the world. While they may have had the sweetest of motivations, they are hampered by a deficient education system which tells them very little about what happens outside America. Is it true that 80% of congressmen have not been outside America? The foreign policy follies coming from the US would suggest that it is.

As I head off into the dark, one of the mature age locals tells me that he has made sure that no one ransacked my boat. Looking back he probably was looking for a tip. What I did was rush back to the boat to see if it was intact. Seemed OK.

Next day I headed across the channel to St Lucia. The current runs two knots to the West. The wind is light and I am making about one knot. You may recall that I point 70^0 off the wind. A day spent jogging across the channel. I have gone further West than North and am feeling a little queasy. I tacked and tried to sail back to St Vincent, but the wind dropped out. So I have a sleep.

Next morning I can see no land. Do I try to tack upwind to get to St Lucia? 'Ah the hell with it.' I head off downwind to Jamaica.

To Jamaica

Now this is an unplanned voyage. On board I have a large bag of rice and a large bag of onions and not much else. I find the sextant, work out the date, sponge the bilges. I found that eating onions without the rice has a dramatic impact on the alimentary canal. Only tried that once.

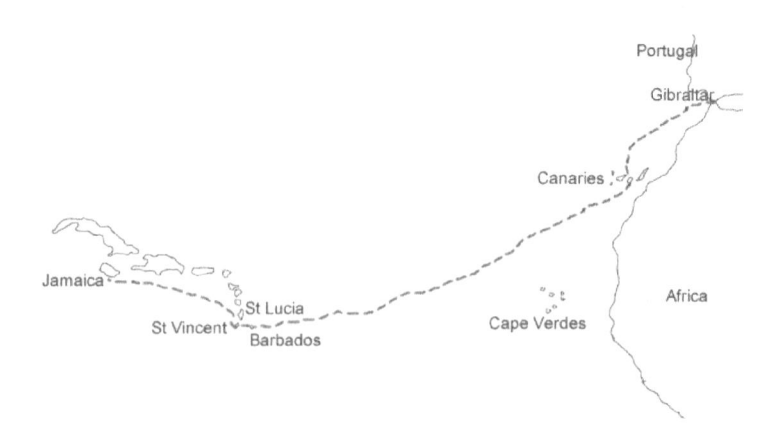

Hove to in order to cook some rice. Have found some tins of vegetables, fewer tins of fruit, at least one tin of ham, one tin of mouldy oats, maybe a tin of sardines and two eggs. Bother - have just broken the arm off my sunglasses.

Wind too light to sail. Two US destroyers passed this morning on their way to Grenada. There was a Canadian destroyer in Kingston for a week while I was there. You may recall that Grenada was an early exercise in regime change.

Am cooking in biscuit tins. Don't have a pot or a pan. Seem to have lost a bucket and a compass in Kingstown. The price of leaving the boat unattended for a week.

Day 5   Good day 3-5 knots all day. Took a wave over the side half an hour before sunset, so halted. Two ships today, two yesterday, four the day before. I was told there were few ships in the Caribbean. Too rough to boil rice.

Day 6   A bad day. Didn't want to sail in the morning and didn't enjoy it all day. Felt hungry and irritable. Stopped three times to cook. First twice too rough for rice, so I cooked thick greasy pancakes. At last have cooked some rice and am feeling lots better. The sea is much larger. Proceeded slowly under jib and mizzen, remembering only too well the 'bows under experience' in the Atlantic.

Day 7 Late morning retired to my locker. Two waves in quick succession have taken control of Donna and nearly rolled her. The second spun her through 180^0. Amusingly, I had just said to myself 'I will either make it in record time or not at all'!

Saw a ship last night on a course to pass astern of me. However his lights kept getting closer and closer. When he was about a mile away scrambled forward raised jib and sailed around his stern. Beating into big seas and strong wind in the dead of night is both wetting and frightening.

Some good days NW, main and mizzen, 2-5 knots and some bad days spent hoven to. Waves too steep to sail. Only about 12 feet, but too steep. (Latitude 16^0 10')

Day 10 Hoven to again. Nearly rolled when a wave crest broke under me. Have put out sea anchor. Two ships last night, both too close for comfort. Second one was circling and closing in. I hid my light. He persisted. I signalled 'D' (I am manoeuvring with difficulty keep clear). He went away.

Vancouver Forest – large timber carrying ship – 200 yards away on Starboard beam when sighted. I need to do a better job of keeping watch.

Light winds not much progress. Made classic Aussie damper (flour and water) for supper last night. Burnt on the outside and runny in the middle, but that's OK. Have eaten a pound of rice today.

Day 13 Good day. Landfall late afternoon. At least two ships last night. Am like a refugee with food. Wolfed tin of ham, two tins of fruit and more rice.

Up at first light gazing at smudge on the horizon. Sailed North towards the coast till early afternoon, thought that I saw Alta Vela. Sailed West until dark. Opened the last tin of Gibraltar oats. They are magnificent. How Asians survive on rice I don't know.

Wondering whether to sail into the coast to make a definitive identification. A French radio station which was close to West is now Close to North. Probably Haiti. Don't want to visit Haiti as I am worried about pirates. Still eating like a horse and longing for the end of this voyage. Just picked up Jamaica radio – weak and West. This land I can see must be Santo Domingo. (Latitude 17⁰ 59')

Day 16 Still becalmed off the coast of Santo Domingo. Had some sea breeze during the night. Used it to get well clear of the coast. Have just made a hat out of some canvas and an old skivvy. Gave my beautiful weather beaten leather hat to Trinidadian Roger in St Vincent. Sun is bloody hot. Have re-read all my mail several times.

Some East wind last night from just after sunset. Sailed SW till after midnight, then sea anchored and slept. Maybe could have left her running W, but still not sure of position and hence uncertain of dangers to the West. Nice conservative strategy. This morning light East wind making half knot West. Had crisp golden fried onions for breckers. (Latitude 17⁰ 55')

Am passing due South of Pte de Gravois (Latitude 18⁰ 01' from the Pilot). This is the first time I have checked a latitude shot against a known point on land. Seems that my calculations are accurate.

Am in what the Polynesians call 'the place where the sea goes up and down'. In the lee of an island where the two swells refracting round either side meet. (Latitude 18⁰ 11') This is about right as I can see Navassa island. Am now heading South of West. Must stay North of Albatross bank. It has some 14 fathom depths. The surrounding sea is 200 fathoms. A 12 foot sea would become 20 foot and more breaking sea over the bank and Donna has had enough punishment without that.

Day 19 Sighted Jamaica mid morning. Think I have identified Yallah's hill and am shaping a course to round it about two miles off. Then into Kingston Harbour. Food, mail, people, smog noise, dirt.

Tacked into Port Morant about two hours after dark. A long way short of Kingston. Quite exciting getting into a strange harbour in the dark with no chart. At one point felt the waves steepen indicating the edge of the reef. Headed out a bit and further along the coast before heading back in towards the harbour.

Am anchored off the jetty in about 30 feet of water. A local offered to protect my boat while I took the bus into Kingston the next day. When I pondered this offer it seemed that my boat and contents were at risk whether I purchased the protection or not. Decided to sail on.

Day 20 Sailed along the coast to Kingston. Got caught in the line to a lobster pot. Brisk breeze, sails all standing, boat wanted to go, but we were being held in one place by the lobster pot line. Managed to cut the line before we turned over or something broke. Proceeded to Kingston and anchored in outer harbour to wait for the customs people.

Took a couple of days for the customs people to appear. Got a message that it was OK to go to the inner harbour and they would clear me later. Didn't believe it. So I waited in the outer harbour. Eventually cleared and sailed into the inner harbour.

As I came in I was accompanied by early finishers in the inaugural Nassau – Kingston ocean yacht race. Went to the presentation night. Most of the owners did not sail. They just flew in to collect the trophy. Seemed to me a bit like owning a greyhound or a very expensive racing pigeon. What satisfaction could this deliver to them? My wallet is bigger than yours! Who cares.

Strolled the streets of Kingston. Wandering through the rough part of town, I saw a group of young men sitting on a wall. As I came level with them one came dancing out and around me brandishing a large carving knife. Looking back, I suppose that I was expected to run or hand over my wallet and watch. What I actually did was smile at him and keep walking.

Lots of the Jamaicans actively resented 'whitey'. I said 'you were never a slave, I was never a slave owner'. It didn't have any effect. These attitudes were not for discussion. Didn't like the idea of being beaten up or worse because of the category I was in rather than something I had done.

I was lunching in the yacht club and asking the people at my table 'how do I get back to Europe'. Yes, at one time I did plan to sail to Australia. However now that I had experienced the power of the waves I was disinclined to undertake another crossing. Someone from an adjacent table said 'see those masts over there, he is looking for crew'. I went and had discussions with the skipper of the barquentine Regina Maris. He offered me the position of Second Officer. I accepted.

Barquentine Regina Maris

A few exciting moments such as being 100 feet up the mast and out on the yard with no safety harness, feet on wobbly chain taking in the sail with both hands, when it was blowing a fair bit more than a gale. If you fell on the deck you would sustain fatal injuries. If you fell in the water they would not be able to find you by the time they turned the ship around. This seemed more dangerous than any part of my voyage.

Forty days later we arrived in Plymouth. The Regina Maris pointed 90 degrees off the wind. We were in sight of Plymouth for two days tacking back and forth waiting for the wind to change before we could get into the harbour.

It had been an interesting experience, however I was anxious to get on with my life, so I headed for London.

After Sailing

When I returned to civilisation I worked for the Digital Equipment Corporation in London leading the introduction of 'mini computers' into banking. These were much cheaper than a comparable 'mainframe' computer. To deliver the turnkey outcome for the banks I teamed up with Hoskyns, Logica and CAP some of the world's finest system houses. We delivered leading edge technology for clients such as Citibank, Lloyds, Rothschilds, Chase Manhattan and the Bank of Kuwait.

The spy who came in

Kerstin invited me to come to Gothenburg for Christmas. I said to my colleagues at Digital 'see you in about ten days' grabbed a taxi straight to Heathrow and took the next plane to Sweden. First we purchased a change of clothes for me, then we celebrated Christmas with the family. One of the few phrases I remember in Swedish is 'clockan tio'. Its ten o'clock. We left the party and headed home. The Swedes are all pagans – candles burning in every window and on graves all across the city. I definitely prefer roast turkey to salt herring.

Now I had been dreaming about Kerstin for a long time. Wonderful dreams. Kerstin was more practical. When my letters arrived full of attempts at poetry, she took them round to the English department at the University and asked if they were any good. We had a delightful time together. I have very sweet recollections. However we realised that this was not the perfect match.

As I was boarding the ferry to return to England, I noticed some coloured condoms. Swedes like to bring some humour to their love life. I purchased a packet of black ones. Later, I consulted some Swedish friends explaining that these condoms were smaller than the English variety and wondering about the credentials of Swedish men. They explained that the ones I had bought in Sweden were for tourists and showed me the condom used by Swedish men. It was a plastic bag which would enclose your arm.

Back in UK I discovered the Rocky Horror Show. It was the original stage show with the sweet transvestite in fish net stockings strutting on the extended stage well into the stalls. Kerstin came to UK to see it. Back then it seemed very progressive.

Went to Wroclaw looking for Stanislav. Seemed to me that the yacht club would be on the river and that they would have heard of him. Was walking on the river bank when I fell into conversation with a local. This is Poland under Russian domination. He would not tell me his name or anything about himself. He took my query of board and my telephone number. About a week later I got a call saying 'I have found him.'

Went back to Wroclaw to catch up with Stanislav. He introduced me to a gorgeous television producer who organised an interview on Polish television about the voyage. Her husband was away, but foolishly I had brought an accomplice with me. I still have the 16mm print. Curious that I have been interviewed on Polish television, but not Australian.

Stanislav would have liked to continue on around the world. His lady friend persuaded him to return. However they had a disagreement about how many men was enough and the relationship ended. Still Poland to Venezuela and back when you start with $10 in your pocket is not bad.

We rented a room in Warsaw from two retired sisters. One had been a nurse, the other a doctor. They told us how the young men from age ten onwards were being raised to be soldiers and throw the Russians out of Poland. They eventually got their wish. I discovered that there are two occasions when the Polish drink:
- one is when it is raining
- the other is when it is not raining!

As the Country Manager for Poland for an English Computer Company – affluent Westerner - I was expected to hand over a bottle of whisky at the commencement of each meeting. The Poles would provide excellent coffee and fresh pretzel sticks. As always, once you understand the conventions life goes on swimmingly. We were in detailed discussion with the Poles about licensing them to manufacture a 16 bit mini computer. There were some problems with ownership of the IP and with COCOM - the committee that approved technology transfers to the Eastern Block.

Our translator was a young Polish woman who spoke her English with a French accent and her French with an English accent. Both countries find this attractive. Very sophisticated.

I drove the 30km North to one of the lakes looking for a sail. The caretaker in the yacht club spoke Polish, Russian and German. I can make myself understood in French and English. Five languages between us but not one in common. However I had money, he had a boat, I went for a sail. No problem.

Driving back to Warsaw I picked up some student hitch hikers. The following weekend they invited me to their place for a party. It was a two room apartment in the industrial sector with two generations living there. 'We hear that Australia has a lot of sheep – is it true?' 'We hear that everyone lives in the bottom right hand corner – is it true?' They knew quite a lot about Australia. More than most Americans for example. However they did not trust their sources and wanted to validate their information. They also wanted to know which one of the students I fancied. I demurred, as I had done lots of hitchhiking myself – giving them a lift was a natural act.

We drank lots of Vodka. Potato pancakes were served to absorb some of the Vodka and enable continued drinking. They would not let me drive home explaining that I would be arrested and put in prison. Further that it was not so easy to get out of prison. The Russian boot was still firmly on the neck of Poland.

Strip tease had only recently been allowed in the night clubs in Warsaw. The performers got their kit off but hadn't really got the hang of the 'tease'. It was like watching the gymnastics at the Olympics as they got their clobber off.

Let me give you a Polish proverb 'life is very brutal and full of Zasadzka'. The Pole who was explaining this to me didn't know the English word for Zasadzka. He said 'you know when John Wayne is riding up to the narrow pass and many people are waiting, 'Life is very brutal and full of ambushes'. Especially if you live on the flat land between Germany and Russia. Maybe more blitzkrieg than ambush.

I believe that Condoleeza Rice, Donald Rumsfeld and Paul Wofowitz know how to pronounce 'nuclear'. I also believe that they inwardly wince when the most powerful man in the world says 'nucular'. Clearly they are not willing to advise him about pronunciation. Makes you worry about what else they are not game to tell him. English is the only language you can speak poorly and yet be taken seriously. Another American contribution to world culture.

A friend sold my boat in Jamaica and informed me that I had some Jamaican dollars available. These were soft dollars, you could not convert them to any other currency. I spent them on air tickets and had a holiday back in Australia. I was looking for somewhere to build a boat. Found the spot. Strahan on the West coast of Tasmania. Close to the source of Huon pine. I had identified a spot where I could do the construction and had begun the negotiation. I imagined chopping the trees down, floating them down the river, getting them milled and then building the boat. A week later all these plans were abandoned when I got married. My love for Europe in undiminished. I will be back.

Because I have some racquet skills I have spent much of my life whacking balls around when I should have been sailing. I have a few trophies including Victorian Amateur Doubles title at Royal Tennis (my partner was in great form), the A Grade Doubles in the Hayman Island Tournament – played in Melbourne (same partner), the inaugural Secretary's Cup at Petworth and C grade champion at the Kerang Easter Lawn Tennis Tournament.

My sweetest recollection of the Royal Melbourne Tennis Club is playing doubles on a Friday afternoon with Ted Cordner and John Snell. A thoroughly civilised and sportsmanlike experience.

This was followed by insightful conversation at the bar with Mike Lindell, Richard Hall and many more. We formed the 'Friday

Knight Champagne Club', sponsored some exhibition matches and tournaments and organised the occasional dinner. Graham Hyland held the crowd spellbound for three hours at one of these with his account of four world championship defences with Wayne Davies.

There were many delightful members in this club. However the human condition expresses itself regardless of income or lineage. There were also some cheats, pretentious prats, employees who abused their position, people who knew how to hold a grudge and people who thought that it was OK to buy the Presidency. I suppose that this is all part of the 'circus of life'. In the contemporary pseudo 'value free' world the villains are those with standards.

Inaugural Secretary's Cup Tournament - Petworth UK

Left to right as follows: Eddie Harrison (club treasurer), Cedric Gunnery, Geoff Stewart, (inaugural winners of the Secretary's Cup competition still played today), Mrs Fleck, S Osmond-Evans (club secretary) and George Cooke (club professional).

Royal Tennis was traditionally a gentleman's game. I first played in England. The standard of play was not great, though utterly gentlemanly in style. The after parties were outstanding with Tatler magazine photographing the gentry at play. Cedric Gunnery and I won the inaugural Secretary's Cup - a doubles tournament with a solid silver trophy. First, rank the players in order of ability, then pair them off starting in the middle. Cedric and I were both near the middle of the list which accounts for the victory.

To the consternation of some, I took my solid silver perpetual trophy back to Australia. At the end of 12 months, I sent the trophy back to Petworth to be hand delivered by Chris Ronaldson who was on his way to becoming world champion. The photograph below now adorns the walls at Petworth.

I played a couple of seasons of village cricket for Lodsworth. There was a great deal of amusing chat in the slips. When the keeper failed to dislodge the bails he was advised that 'it was like courting, you've got to get them off'.

We went to the annual Horn Fair at Charlton in Kent with a cricket match, diverse entertainments and an athletics competitions for the kids. The local squire donated a ewe and a ram for the event. The animals were roasted on a spit and the horns were mounted on a trophy. This 'prowess' trophy was given to the batsman who made the most runs. Everyone with any connection with this village returned for the weekend. I continue to believe that we all need the identity, interaction and intimacy that comes from being part of a village.

Cruising with son Ben

Since then I have spent decades shovelling my way through the trivia of everyday life. It is definitely time to cross another ocean. Every time I sail and feel the boat lift to the sea I feel profoundly happy.

This summer I sailed a Yachting World Diamond. An oldie, but a goodie.

We had an immense amount of fun as you can see from the pictures. I have now sold this boat and am looking for something that can handle an ocean crossing.

A Sunday afternoon

It is my view that a gentleman should neither sail against the wind nor encourage the sociopathic, reptilian 'winning is everything' mentality. Let the people who want to shout at one another go racing.

Are we having fun yet?

Yes 'barging' is against the rules and it is unsportsmanlike. Was there a time when Commodores of yacht clubs took responsibility for ensuring civilised behaviour in the racing fleet?

That is why lots of us prefer to go cruising. For an elegant exploration of the 'winning is everything' approach to life may I suggest a French movie entitled 'Manon des Sources'.

Now I have five children and am single again. The Polish word for bachelor is Cavalier. Sounds much more romantic don't you think. Here are the two little ones.

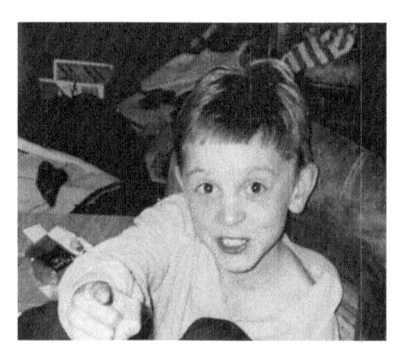

This is Cleopatre Julia aged 9 and Lancelot Angus aged 10

Am planning to buy or build an ocean going boat and get back to the Baltic and the Med. This is a reprise of my plans from 30 years ago. There is a festival on Gotland in August each year celebrating the Viking voyaging and trading culture of 1000 years ago. I plan to sail to Petersburg and explore the Hermitage. Also on the list are the Balearics, Corsica, Sardinia, Malta the Greek Islands and Constantinople. Let's not forget the Azores, the Canaries, and the Caribbean. Island people are more friendly.

I have a copy of 'Ocean Passages for the World' by my bed and often check out distances, winds and currents etc. On my way back to Europe, I will skip the Red Sea because of pirates, that leaves Cape Horn or the Cape of Good Hope. Neither attractive, but probably prefer the latter – not so cold. I have spent six months checking the weather on the Web every day at both Cape Horn and the Cape of Good Hope.

I quite like the strategy followed by the square riggers approaching Cape Horn – stay around forty across the Pacific (at the top edge of the lows where the wind goes in the right direction). Then about 300 miles from the Cape follow the Albatross strategy of heading South on the front edge of a low. Gives you a couple of days to get a sun shot before you hit the 70 mile wide gap South of the Horn.

In the days of the square riggers, sailors who had rounded the Horn were entitled to wear an earing. Wonder if Andre Agassi has rounded the Horn?

The Cape of Good Hope also known as the 'Cape of Storms' is where the warm Agulhas current going South down the East coast of Africa at two to four knots meets the cold Westerly prevailing wind and current in the roaring forties. Has been known to get a bit lumpy. Recently I have been checking the weather here. There were two weeks in mid January that looked OK.

Sometime soon I must stop this armchair voyaging and head out to sea. Probably time that you did the same. See you out there.

Documents

000100

PORT OF GIBRALTAR

Pratique Note

The *Aus. M.␣ Sora Eloisa*
whereof *J. Stewart* is the Master,
with *Nil* crew and _____ passengers,
arrived 20 / 2 / 19 73 is admitted to pratique.

PORT RULES

20. (1) Every vessel shall occupy the berth assigned to her by the Captain of the Port whether at a quay or elsewhere, and shall be removed to any other berth which the Captain of the Port may direct; and the master or person in charge of any vessel at all times shall obey the directions of the Captain of the Port.

30. (3) All ships alongside in the Port shall affix efficient rat guards on every line and wire connected to or reaching the shore.

In pursuance of Port Rule 20 (1) above, you are hereby directed to berth in the following position :-

Berth _____

*Boarding Officer
for Captain of the Port.*

A fine of £100 is laid down for each stowaway landed without the permission of the Commissioner of Police.

Masters are warned against allowing oil, oil sullage, dirt, bilge water or other filth to be discharged into the Bay. The law provides for heavy penalties.

P.T.O.

INVOICE

HONNOR MARINE LTD
DIRECTORS: L CHURCHOUSE · [illegible] WESTELL · F H GUEST

Yacht and Boat Builders

SEYMOUR WHARF
TOTNES · DEVON
ENGLAND TQ9 5AJ
TELEPHONE: TOTNES 2229 (STD code 080465)

Mr. Rowe,
Bank of N.S.W.,
Collins Street,
Melbourne,
Victoria,
Australia.

V.A.T. Reg. No. 140 9806 69

No. M.68

DATE 3rd October, 1973

Galvanised Longboat rudder complete with tiller		£12.75
12 sets of parell beads		6.00
Starboard rear rowlock block		1.00
Two galvanised steel rudder guides complete with fastenings		2.50
Carriage and packing by Air Freight to Las Palmas		16.00
		£38.25

Despatched by Air Freight to:- Mr. G. W. Stewart,
c/o Harbourmaster,
Las Palmas,
Gran Canaria.

REAL CLUB NAUTICO DE
GRAN CANARIA
LAS PALMAS

SR STEWART

NAME OF THE YATCH DONNA ELVIRA

VALID FROM 17-10-73
TO 24-10-73

ONLY FOR
USE THE
ANCHORING-
GROUND

SANDRINGHAM YACHT CLUB
A MEMBER CLUB OF THE VICTORIAN YACHTING COUNCIL

TELEPHONES:
OFFICE 598 7003 598 2795
AFTER HOURS: STEWARDS
598 7003 598 5546

JETTY ROAD, SANDRINGHAM P.O. BOX 3, SANDRINGHAM, 3191
Please address all communications to THE SECRETARY

15th December, 1977.

Mr. G.W. Stewart,
3 Bellaire Court,
TOORAK.   3142.

Dear Sir,

Your letter concerning the formation an association of cruising yachtsmen was received on 21-11-77 and I submitted it to the next meeting of my General Committee which was held last night.

In addition to displaying your letter on the notice board, I have been authorised to have it published in our magazine "Off the Wind" which goes to some 1500 members and we will suggest that, if anyone is interested, they should contact you direct.

Best wishes for a successful venture.

Yours faithfully,

Fred. C. Pain
Secretary

Glossary

aback – Normally you are harnessing the wind to go where you want. Sometimes the waves turn the boat around or the wind changes direction so that the wind blows on the wrong side of the sails. This is called having the sails aback.

Aegre – small yacht sailed by Nick and Julie Grainger see – http://www.mavc2002.com/caledoniayawl/aegresum.htm

aground – boat stuck in the mud or on the rocks.

all standing – when all sails are up and full of wind.

Auld Alliance – alliance between France and Scotland.

backing plates – metal plates like giant washers to strengthen the surface to which the fitting is attached.

beacon – could be a radio station or a navigational beacon, source of signal to assist with navigation.

beating – sailing the zig zag course against the wind.

bilges – bottom of the inside of the boat where water accumulates.

block and tackle – pulleys and wheels to make lifting easier.

bombora – area where waves are higher than the water is deep.

bottled – the boat turning upside down.

boulangerie – bread shop.

boule – French game of bowls played with iron balls and wooden jack.

bon appetit – enjoy your meal.

bow – pointy end of boat.

broach – boat turning sideways.

broad reaching – sailing across the wind.

browns – the normal triangular sails, jib, main and mizzen.

bucolic - of or characteristic of shepherds or flocks; pastoral.

bully beef – canned beef or ordinary quality.

bumpkin – length of wood extending from the stern of the boat to which mizzen sheet was attached.

calypso - A type of music that originated in the West Indies, notably in Trinidad, and is characterised by improvised lyrics on topical or broadly humorous subjects.

Canaries – The Canary Islands.

capsize – turning upside down.

C'est la vie – who cares.

Chalombiers – people who live on and work the barges in the French canals.

chanter – something like the musical instrument called a recorder, but used for practising the bag pipes.

Chooks – fowl, hens, feathered egg laying, flying beasties.

chronometer – accurate clock used for navigation.

chuffed – extraordinarily pleased.

cloud seeding – dropping chemicals onto the clouds in an attempt to produce rain.

come in green – a wave which comes on board as solid water rather than spray.

cooba libra – rum and coke.

damper – simple Australian bread substitute made of flour and water and often baked on a camp fire.

defecation – number 2, going to the toilet.

detritus - disintegrated or eroded matter. Accumulated material; debris.

deux chevaux – literally two horses, usually applied to a small French car.

deviation card – description of the discrepancy between what your compass does and what it should do.

dingy – very small boat for rowing.

dock – pier.

doldrums – area near the equator with light and variable winds – also known as the horse latitudes as the horses would be thrown overboard when the food ran out.

dorado – ocean fish 2 to 4 ft long.

dork – someone who is not cool.

elysian - Blissful; delightful.

emblematic - of, relating to, or serving as an emblem; symbolic.

excrement – fruit of defecation.

fisherman's anchor – traditional looking anchor with two big hooks.

flood - See http://www.accuracyingenesis.com/flood.html for further information.

freeboard – distance from the water to the edge of the boat.

frugal – using as little as possible.

gash – hash, marijuana.

Grand Flute - stretch baguette.

greens – square sails 8ft by 4 ft.

gunter – mast extension.

gunwale – top edge of boat.

gymbals – double hinged arrangement to keep things flat while the boat moved about eg. the kettle on the stove.
halyard – line for hauling the sails up.
hanked on jib – hooked the edge of the jib to the forestay.
headsail – jib, triangular sail at the front of the boat.
HORN FAIR. An annual fair held at Charlton, in Kent, on St. Luke's day, the 18th of October. It consists of a riotous mob, who after a printed summons dispersed through the adjacent towns, meet at Cuckold's Point, near Deptford, and march from thence in p. Source: 1811 Dictionary of the Vulgar Tongue.
hundreds and thousands – coloured sugary granules for cake decoration.
Illich – Ivan Illich radical education reformer ex Catholic Priest see http://www.cogsci.ed.ac.uk/~ira/illich/
jerry – toilet.
jerry can – four gallon container.
jetties – pier, dock.
jib – small triangular sail at the front of the boat.
Ken Duxbury – Lugworm on the loose.
knot – unit of speed, one nautical mile per hour.
langlauf – cross country skiing.
lash the helm – put a rope around the helm to keep it in position.
lee shore – a piece of land towards which the wind is blowing.
light ship – a light house on the sea, boat anchored in fixed position displaying lights to aid navigation.
littoral - the region or zone between the limits of high and low tides.
lock – section of canal with gates at both ends to allow boats to be floated up or down to meet the level of the next section of the canal.
Madeira – Island off the coast of Spain.
main – main sail, the big one aft of the main mast.
Marseillan - http://www.pernic.co.uk/
Med – the Mediterranean Sea.
merci Dieu – Thanks be to God.
mizzen – small sail at the stern of the boat.
Nautical Tables – book full of numbers to allow the sextant reading to be translated into the Latitude.
newfies – people from Newfoundland.
Nimzowitsch – author on chess.

Norman Davies - The Isles – A History, Norman Davies, Oxford, p.1043

olfactory - to do with sniffing.

pain chocolat - chocolate croissants.

Paleomagnetic dating –
>   http://www.ga.gov.au/odp/publications/173_SR/chap_08/c8_2.htm

parell beads – spherical wooden beads threaded on a line, used to hook the gunter to the mast, so that it can move up and down.

pick – anchor.

Pilot – The Pilot Book which describes navigational matters for a particular area.

pintles – guides into which the rudder was slotted.

pitchpoled – a forward somersault of the boat.

Polaris - as Polaris is directly above the North Pole, the angle of Polaris to the horizon gives you your Latitude.

poms – puffed up English people.

port – left hand side of the boat looking forward.

prating - to talk idly and at length; chatter.

quel domage – tough tit.

radar reflector - should make me look like a battleship on their radar screen.

rations – provisions, food.

reaching – travelling across the wind.

retsina – Greek wine with pine flavour.

running backstay – extra line from the mast to the stern of the boat to strengthen the mast.

sailing directions – navigational instructions on how to get from one place to another.

sails all standing – all sails up.

sea anchor – canvas sack on end of rope to stop the boat blowing down wind.

seaworthiness - Seaworthiness the Forgotten Factor, C. A. Marchaj, Tiller 1986 & 1996

Sextant – mechanical device with filters and mirrors used to obtain the angle between the horizon and the sun.

shrouds – heavy lines which hold the mast up.

skeg – skinny keel.

siblings – related sprogs.

sight – the number which results from the use of the sextant.

sippets – fried squares of bread.

skin fittings – holes in the hull of the boat, for example where the engine water inlet is connected.
smidge – tiny bit.
spar – length of wood.
sporran – funny furry bit on the front of the kilt.
squall – moments of stronger wind.
squares – Square sails.
starboard – Right hand side of the boat looking forward.
steerage – when the boat is going fast enough to be steered.
stick – mast.
stem head – metal fitting on the pointy end of the boat.
stern – back end of boat.
strand – rope unwinding into its constituent parts.
superior square sail – uppermost square sail.
taffrail log – line with spinner on the end trailed over the stern of the ship to estimate distance travelled.
taking a sight – using the sextant to get the angle between the sun and the horizon.
telltale compass – compass inside the cabin.
tender – easy to wobble.
test match – international cricket match.
Thurber – James Thurber, US humorist.
tilley lantern – kerosene burning pressure lantern.
tribology - The science of the mechanisms of friction, lubrication, and wear of interacting surfaces that are in relative motion.
trimmed – sail trim.
twin forestays – two forestays so that one can attach two jibs.
unbent – taking the sails off.
whitehorses – braking waves.
wind shadow – area near to land where there is no wind.
yaw – rotational motion around a vertical axis.

Planning an Ocean Crossing

Bruce Gaynham of the World Cruising Club said to me a few days ago 'To think of all the equipment and paraphernalia that the boats have onboard these days to do the crossing, and how little you had!'

The WCC cruise from the Canaries to St Lucia in 2004 departed on 21 November with 190 yachts from 23 countries. www.worldcruising.com

Now I know that crossing in an open boat is very different from a crossing in a large ocean going yacht. You may have all of these issues covered. However just in case, I offer a couple of fundamental ideas for your consideration.

My concern is that in the drive for speed and windward performance we may have overlooked some issues relating to seaworthiness.

Remember that your life is on the line here. You screw up you die.

To quote Kipling from the Harp Song of the Dane Women

What is a woman that you forsake her,
And the hearth fire and the home acre,
To go with the old grey Widow-maker?

Have you thought about what happens when:
- the electrics fail
- the skeg falls off
- the mast comes down
- the boat fills with water
- Rudder breaks
- Hit by a ship
- Heart attack
- Tall sticks
- Crew

The details are on the web site:
www.sailsouthtillthebuttermelts.com

Ordering Information

Bookshops selling Sail South till the butter melts are listed at:

www.sailsouthtillthebuttermelts.com

Book Sellers

Details are listed on Bowkerlink. Further information available from info@thecontinuitycompany.com.au
Orders to orders@thecontinuitycompany.com.au or by mail to
The Continuity Company
Box 211, Camberwell, Victoria 3124 Australia

Signed copy of the Second Edition

You can order a copy of the second edition signed by the author. You may suggest the wording for a salutation if you wish.

See details at:
www.sailsouthtillthebuttermelts.com

Signed copy of the First Edition

There are still a few copies of the first edition signed by the author available. You may suggest the wording for a salutation if you wish.

See details at:
www.sailsouthtillthebuttermelts.com

If all else fails

If you have trouble getting a copy of the book just email me:

gwstewart@sailsouthtillthebuttermelts.com

and we will get something organised.